ABOUT THE AUTHOR

Simon Tupman, MBA, APS, Solicitor (Eng & Wales)

Simon Tupman is the Director of Simon Tupman Presentations, the organisation he founded in 1994 to provide professional practices with the business knowledge and motivation needed to counter the challenges of change and competition. Since then, the organisation has built up an extensive client base across a range of industries, notably the legal profession.

The author started professional life as a solicitor in England in the mid-1980s. After post-graduate studies in London, he turned his world upside down (literally) by moving to New Zealand in 1992. After spending two years as an in-house marketing manager for a 21-partner law firm, he established his own business. In 1997, he moved the business to Australia to work with a wider range of organisations.

His presentations are renowned for their practical, relevant, entertaining and inspiring information.

If you are interested in having Simon Tupman address your organisation, please call (612) 6680 9991.

ADVANCE PRAISE FOR *WHY LAWYERS SHOULD EAT BANANAS*

"This book is filled with deceptively simple but truly profound 'home-truths'. Reading it challenges you to think about what you are doing with your career and your life."
David Maister, the world's leading authority on professional service firm management and author of *True Professionalism* and *Managing The Professional Service Firm*, Boston, USA

"If someone had have given me this to read 10 or 15 years ago, my life as a partner would probably have been more fun. It should be mandatory reading, especially for undergraduates before they take the plunge."
John Chisholm, CEO, Middletons Moore & Bevins, Melbourne, Australia

"Simon has provided a refreshingly honest look at our lives as lawyers, and offers some timely ideas and advice in an easy to read book on how we can obtain a higher level of satisfaction from our professional life and a much better balance with life outside work."
Adrian Aherne, Managing Partner, Andersen Legal, Sydney, Australia

"How superb to find a book which helps lawyers take control of their own destinies— and how timely. It's also good to find a book that is easy to read as well as actually being practical in its approach."
Meredith Hellicar, CEO, Corrs Chambers Westgarth, Sydney, Australia

"Entertaining and insightful. Recommended to lawyers and other primates with something to say or sell…"
Robert Pay, Managing Director, Jaffe Associates, Europe
Former Head of Marketing, Cifford Chance and London Stock Exchange

"Simon's book is a 'straight from the heart', intelligent and comprehensive insight into how lawyers can improve their quality of life. It will inspire change and understanding in every reader—lawyer and non-lawyer alike."
David Connor, Partner, Hesketh Henry, Auckland, New Zealand

"Everything Simon says makes sense and will make you money. Read this book, prosper…and live longer too!"
Winston Marsh, International Business Authority, Business Growth Centre, Melbourne, Australia

"I commend this book to my colleagues as a means of reflection of what we started at the outset of our careers, where we have travelled, and where we might go for greater professional and personal fulfilment."
Paul K. Cooper, Managing Director, The LAAMS Group Of Continuing Legal Education & Publishing Companies, Sydney, Australia

"Whether you are the senior partner or just taking the first steps in your legal career, this book is full of valuable self-help instruction and insights. A 'fruitful read'!"
Richard Johnstone, Partner, Wynn Williams & Co, Christchurch, New Zealand

"Simon has written a humane and very practical book. It is a reminder that we are human beings first and lawyers second and that we can only reach our full potential as lawyers when we are attentive to our own human needs and those of our colleagues and clients. Simon's excellent tips are but the further expression of this idea."
Danny Gilbert, Managing Partner, Gilbert & Tobin, Sydney, Australia

Why Lawyers Should Eat Bananas

INSPIRATIONAL IDEAS FOR LAWYERS
WANTING MORE OUT OF LIFE

To Ed & Judy,

With love,

Simon

x

SIMON TUPMAN

National Library of Australia
Cataloguing–in-Publication Entry:

    Tupman, Simon.
    Why lawyers should eat bananas : inspirational ideas for
    lawyers wanting more out of life.

    Bibliography.
    ISBN 0 646 40432 6.

    1. Lawyers - Conduct of life. 2. Life skills. I. Title.

    340.092

ISBN 0 646 40432 6

First published November 2000

Printed in Australia by: Australian Print Group, Maryborough, Victoria
Cartoon illustrations by Wayne Logue, PO Box 36523, Auckland, New Zealand
Design and layout by Sharon McGrath, Buzzard Wings (02) 6684 3394
Edited by Sally Macmillan (02) 9979 3025

Published by Simon Tupman Presentations Pty Ltd (ABN 54 088 337 884)
PO Box 159, Byron Bay, NSW 2481, Australia
Telephone: (02) 6680 9991 Fax: (02) 6680 9992
Email: stupman@ozemail.com.au
Website: www.simontupman.com.au

The purpose of this book is to educate and to provide knowledge and information in regard to the subject matter covered. Every care has been taken to ensure the accuracy of the material contained herein at the time of publication. Neither the author nor Simon Tupman Presentations Pty Ltd assumes any responsibility for errors, omissions or contrary interpretation of the subject matter herein. Adherence to all applicable rules and regulations governing business practices, advertising and all other aspects of doing business in jurisdictions throughout the world is the sole responsibility of the reader. Neither the author nor Simon Tupman Presentations Pty Ltd can guarantee the results that readers may or may not get as a result of following the ideas outlined in this book.

CONTENTS

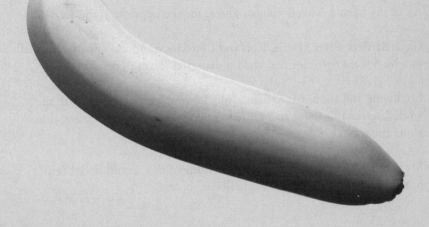

ACKNOWLEDGMENTS

To the many people who have contributed to the development of this book, thank you all. You know who you are. Family, friends, clients and professional colleagues, you have all made this possible. In particular, I must acknowledge:

Dottie Walters, David Maister, Dr David Freemantle, Robyn Henderson, Keith Abraham, Cyndi Kaplan, Winston Marsh, Dr Alan Kemp, Peter Hughman, Peter Black, Dr Deepak Chopra, Dr Shiv Mathur, W. Mitchell, Marilynne Burton, Ann Andrews, Ed Bernacki and Karen Beard, all of whom have inspired me, taught me or both!

Rod McGeoch, Pat O'Shane, Carmen Argibay, Larry Schreiter, James O'Loghlin, Deborah Zurnamer, John Clark, Ross Holmes and Evelyn Ashley for their rich contributions.

My editor, Sally Macmillan, for her tireless support, energy and enthusiasm. Your friendship is a treasure.

The designer of this book, Sharon McGrath, for her creativity and selfless professionalism. I love your work!

All of my clients. Thank you for giving me the opportunity to learn.

Gaye Bartlett, Peter Harris, Rob and Lou Mounsey, and Gina Collins, all of whom were there for me when it mattered. Thank you all.

My loving and supportive friend, Julie Davies, for putting up with me while I wrote this book and for helping me through many testing times along the way.

My mother, Margaret, without whom none of this would have been possible. Thank you for always believing in me.

To my family, who support me in everything that I do.

PERMISSIONS

The following organisations and individuals were kind enough to give permission for the reproduction of previously published material:

Virgin Publishing: extract from *Losing My Virginity* by Sir Richard Branson on pages 95 and 96

David Maister: extracts from *True Professionalism*

Dr Alan Weiss: extracts from *Million Dollar Consulting*

Dr David Freemantle: extracts from *The 80 Things You Must Do to Be a Really Great Boss* and *What Customers Like About You*

Keith Abraham: extract from *Creating Loyal Profitable Customers*

Every effort has been made to ensure that correct attribution has been given to all sources used in this book. The author, publisher, or editor cannot take responsibility for any errors or omissions, but would be grateful to receive any notifications of corrections. Sources not given appropriate credit will be included in future editions.

Introduction

Byron Bay, New South Wales, Australia

Once upon a time, I was a criminal defence lawyer in London. By 1988, having been in practice for nearly five years, I realised I was not enjoying my career very much. I knew what I didn't want to do but I didn't know what I did want to do. Eventually, I decided to return to university to start full-time post-graduate studies in the hope that they would equip me with new skills and present new opportunities. Fortunately, they did and for the following two years I worked in an entirely new role—as a marketing consultant with one of London's leading advertising agencies.

I can recall several people trying to dissuade me from giving up the law; one person suggested that my decision was a terrible waste, especially after all the studying and the years invested in my career. I disagree. It was anything but a waste. My legal training has without doubt been the solid foundation upon which I have been able to build my new career—consulting and speaking to people in business, helping them to become more successful personally and professionally.

It was probably the best decision I ever made, because it put me on a path that has forced me to develop my knowledge and skills; it has enabled me to pursue interests that I enjoy and to discover a more balanced life.

After a couple of years spent at the advertising agency, an opportunity arose to move to New Zealand. I could have played it safe, stayed in the job and settled for what I thought of at the time as financial security. However, in spite of the apparent risk involved, I felt that this was a golden opportunity not to be passed up lightly. With no job and just £1,000 in my pocket, I decided to turn my world upside down—literally!

Not long after I arrived in New Zealand, I took up a position as the first ever marketing manager of a 21-partner law practice. I will always be grateful to them for having the courage not only to create that position but also to select me from other candidates, and then to allow me to carry out some ground-breaking work.

Two years later, in 1994, I suffered an entrepreneurial seizure and decided to set up my own business. Since then, I have made many mistakes but I have also learnt much about the importance of establishing personal and professional priorities. I have also had the opportunity to learn a great deal about how law firms think about their business, having been in the privileged position of working with a range of firms throughout Australia and New Zealand. They have all given me the chance to learn about their businesses, through their clients and their people, and to introduce some new ways of thinking into those firms.

Much of what I have learnt has also come from the many books I have read, the seminars I have attended and the tapes I have listened to. The contribution made by my mentors within the International Federation of Professional Speakers has also been significant.

Making changes to my career and my life was not an easy option. Some people tell me I am lucky to have escaped the law and the city and to live in a special part of the world. Fortunate perhaps, but not lucky. We all have choices in life as well as decisions to make. I made mine at a time when it seemed right for me to do so. Some of those decisions were difficult, and could not have been made confidently without the encouragement of my friends and especially the love and support of my family. However, I do believe that had I not responded to the little voice inside me, I may well have continued down a path to unhappiness and professional dissatisfaction.

In writing this book, I have highlighted the most relevant ideas that I believe will make a powerful contribution to the success of your practice and to your professional life. I hope they challenge you to think about the quality of your professional life and to make the necessary improvements and adjustments so you will enjoy it more.

As I was writing this book, I asked a lawyer friend what was the biggest professional challenge he was facing. He replied that he was grappling with four:

First, how to escape from the concept that he is selling time;

Second, how to create relationships with clients whereby they treat him as a partner in the solution process rather than a guarantor of the solution;

Third, how to deal with the stress of court work brought on by clients who fail to appreciate what they are getting themselves into;

Fourth; learning how to prioritise and limit the time that he devotes to practising law. As he put it: "I am a human being that practises law, not a lawyer that practises being a human being."

If you understand where he's coming from, then you will find material in this book to help you approach and overcome these challenges and restore your self-confidence, sense of purpose and enjoyment of your professional life.

If you are in partnership, some of the ideas may require consensus among your partners in order to be implemented. Large partnerships, in particular, tend to be very institutional so these ideas will challenge some of their traditional thinking and practices, notably the concept of selling value rather than time. Nevertheless, most of the ideas are for individual consumption and can be implemented without crippling expense. To make it happen though, you must want to make some changes to improve your working life and you must be committed to following through.

Finally, I have always learnt from the thoughts and attitudes of other people who have been successful. As a result, I set out to identify a group of lawyers or ex-lawyers who are different or who are making a difference to society and who hold strong views about the legal profession. Their comments are included. I thank all of them for their support and participation in helping me complete this book.

Please treat this book as your personal guide to making a difference to the lives of your clients, your colleagues, but most of all, to your own life.

Enjoy reading it and then living it.

CHAPTER 1

The Way of the World

"The world is moving so fast these days that
the man who says it can't be done
is generally interrupted by someone doing it."

HARRY EMERSON FOSDICK

H ow did your world look today? Did you leap out of bed this morning and go for some exercise? Did you smile at yourself in the bathroom mirror? Did you eat a healthy breakfast? Were you able to delegate your work to younger colleagues while you used your precious time to do something you love doing, perhaps playing with the kids, making love to your partner, playing golf, going fishing or sailing, reading a book, working with a charity, or simply making someone's day? If you did, congratulations. For many readers though, this scenario may seem improbable, even impossible!

A PROFESSION IN CRISIS

I would imagine that you probably cursed the alarm clock, regretted the last drink you had before you went to bed, slipped reluctantly into your work clothes, forgot breakfast, got delayed in the commuter rush, dealt with office politics and then had a meeting with the client from hell. By the time 6pm arrived, you were exhausted. You wondered how you only managed to bill 3.2 hours, and to relieve the tension, you decided to have a drink or two.

Does that sound more like your day? Well if it does, you are not alone. Recent research from various sources suggests that:

✓ 70% of lawyers say they would start a new career if they could
✓ One in three lawyers are dissatisfied with their working life
✓ Lawyers have the highest incidence of depression among 105 leading occupations
✓ 75% of lawyers suffer from work-related stress
✓ Three areas most lawyers identified as causing work related stress are:
  (i) too much work
  (ii) not enough time for family or social life
  (iii) excessively long hours.

These figures suggest a profession in some sort of crisis.

A PROFESSION UNDER FIRE

In 1997, *The Sydney Morning Herald* published an editorial headed "The Greed of Lawyers", quoting the New South Wales Director of Public Prosecutions, Nicholas Cowdery QC. It read:

"*In a new age of economic rationalism, firms pursue profit and measure the performance—the worth of their lawyers by the profit they generate. The public worth of a barrister is measured by the fees commanded. Rewards depend on profit, not on the quality of service—insurance companies cover lapses in that area."*

The editorial added its own comment: "This is a sorry picture but true. It is just as well that the best lawyers want to change it."

Economic rationalism has created a pressure-cooker environment. Large firm management thinking seems to place emphasis on financial achievement ahead of other values and interests. Some would argue that the pressures go with the territory. This may be true but is that a justification for upholding a system that promotes such a crisis?

Thankfully, this problem is now more openly acknowledged and it seems the profession now wants to take steps to do something about it. Recently, in his monthly column in the *Law Institute Journal*, Michael Gawler, President of the Law Institute of Victoria, wrote:

> *"To my mind, top tier firms owe a duty to their staff and to the profession, to lead by example. Employees will continue to attempt to impress their partners and managers by working longer and billing more than each other. They have no capacity to limit that competition beyond their own mature judgment. By contrast, the big firms do have the capacity to change the culture of their workplaces by limiting employee work time, by ensuring that leave is taken and by being brave enough to recognise the value of looking after their staff and to balance that value against the demands of clients."*

Mr Gawler is essentially right. I would add that firms have to be brave enough to recognise the value of looking after not only their staff but also their clients and to balance that value against the demands of the profit and loss account. Large firms are often slow to change. Everyone seems to wait for the other person to make the first move. Why shouldn't it be you?

It is possible to create the type of day you want and the type of lifestyle you want around your practice without waiting for firm policy. Open up your mind, dream a little and when you've finished, take steps to put some of the ideas into practice. No matter how strong your resolve may be to change things, nothing will happen unless you make it happen. Let's make a start.

IT'S ALL ABOUT CHOICES

First, consider these important questions:

- Are you happy in your job?
- Do you enjoy the work you are doing?
- Do you like the clients you advise?
- Are you a confident communicator and delegator?
- Do you have enough free time?
- Do your clients rave about you and refer you freely?
- Do you get enough rewards from your work?

When I was a lawyer, I would have answered no to these questions. As a result, I chose to pursue a career outside the law. If that is what will bring you fulfilment in your life, you must seriously consider it. If law is your calling but you want to make your life more enjoyable, then this book will help you. It's your choice.

Obviously, the older you are, or the more successful you may appear, the harder it may be to make changes to your life. However, it can be done. Your life is not just the result of the choices you make; it's equally the result of those you don't make. You can change things if you want to.

WHAT HAS CHANGED?

Many senior lawyers these days comment that the legal profession is not what it used to be. We live in an increasingly litigious society where there are more lawyers eager to take advantage of society's appetite for making a buck in court. What has changed? Consider first these words:

"I am not an accomplished lawyer. I find quite as much material for a lecture in those points wherein I have failed, as in those wherein I have been moderately successful. The leading rule for the lawyer, as for the man of every other calling, is diligence. Leave nothing for tomorrow that can be done today. Never let your correspondence fall behind. Whatever piece of business you have in hand, before stopping, do all the labour pertaining to it which can then be done. When you bring a common law suit, if you have the facts for doing

so, write the declaration at once. If a law point be involved examine the books and note the authority you rely on upon the declaration itself, where you are sure to find it when wanted. The same of defences and pleas. In business not likely to be litigated—ordinary collection cases, foreclosures, partitions and the like—make all examinations of titles and note them and even draft orders and decrees in advance. This course has a triple advantage; it avoids omissions and neglect, saves you labour when done, performs the labour out of court when you have leisure, rather than in court when you have not. Extemporaneous speaking should be practised and cultivated. It is the lawyer's avenue to the public. However able and faithful he may be in other respects, people are slow to bring him business if he cannot make a speech. And yet there is not a more fatal error to young lawyers than relying too much on speech making. If anyone, upon his rare powers of speaking, shall claim an exemption from the drudgery of the law, his case is a failure in advance.

"Discourage litigation. Persuade your neighbours to compromise whenever you can. Point out to them how the nominal winner is often a real loser—in fees, expenses, and a waste of time. As a peacemaker, the lawyer has a superior opportunity of being a good man. There will still be business enough.

"Never stir up litigation. A worse man can scarcely be found than one who does this. Who can be more nearly a friend than he who habitually overhauled the register of deeds in search of defects in title, whereon to stir up strife and put money in his pocket? A moral tone ought to be infused into the profession which should drive such men out of it.

"The matter of fees is important, far beyond the mere question of bread and butter involved. Properly attended to, fuller justice is done to both lawyer and client. An exorbitant fee should never be claimed. As a general rule never take your whole fee in advance, nor any more than a small retainer. When fully paid beforehand, you are more than a common mortal if you can feel the same interest in the case, as if something was still in prospect for you, as well as your client. And when you lack interest in the case, the job *will very likely lack skill and diligence in the performance. Settle the amount of the fee and take a note in advance. Then you will feel that you are working for something and you are sure to do your work faithfully and well. Never sell a fee note, at least not before the consideration service is performed. It leads to negligence and dishonesty; negligence by losing interest in the case and dishonesty in refusing to refund when you have allowed the consideration to fail.*

"There is a vague popular belief that lawyers are necessarily dishonest. I say vague, because when we consider to what extent confidence and honours are reposed in and conferred upon lawyers by the people, it appears improbable that their impression of dishonesty is very distinct and vivid. Yet the impression is common, almost universal. Let no young man choosing the law for his calling for a moment yield to that popular belief—resolve to be honest at all events; and if in your own judgment you cannot be an honest lawyer, resolve to be honest without being a lawyer. Choose some other occupation rather than one in the choosing of which you do, in advance, consent to be a knave."

ABRAHAM LINCOLN, ESSAY, 1850

In today's fast-paced world, Lincoln's advice remains timely. The world changes and lawyers must change with the times. However, it doesn't mean that this has to be at the expense of their values or principles. Otherwise, they sell their soul.

As recently as the late 1970s, when I was embarking on my legal career in Britain, I was told that I was entering a profession that was stable and secure because the world would always need lawyers. That advice seemed accurate at the time. I recall making decisions for many reasons, most of them having little to do with my own contentment. Since then, the world has changed; economic reforms that led to worldwide programs of privatisation and deregulation eventually had their impact on the legal profession, blowing down the doors of many inefficient and protectionist-minded regulatory bodies and firms. Just think about some of the recent developments:

- The world is getting smaller. Worldwide firms are now the rule rather than the exception. The trend towards global firms is being driven by global clients who want to deal with one firm offering a wide range of services, including accounting, legal and financial. In other words, a one-stop shop.

- The number of lawyers around the world is growing rapidly; in the past 50 years in the US alone, there has been an increase from 200,000 attorneys to 1,000,000.

- Traditional areas of work are now being performed by accountants, consultants, conveyancers, collection agencies and real estate agents. Currently, accountants in the US are estimated to have a $2-$3 billion dollar share in a market worth $70-$80 billion. It has been predicted that accountants will own up to 30% of the legal market by 2008.

- The rich are getting richer and the poor are getting poorer. Recently, it was predicted that Australia would end up with a legal elite who would compete for international work and that partners' salaries would be in excess of $1 million a year. Conversely, those firms who lose out to the bigger firms may find it all too hard and sell out to the bigger firms.

- Technology continues to transform how lawyers transact business; legal software is readily available off the shelf and off the Internet; laptops are changing how lawyers operate and the speed in which matters are resolved.

- Clients are becoming increasingly choosy and demanding, with many major companies cutting the number of law firm suppliers.

- Mediation and arbitration has become a growth area that is replacing traditional litigation.

- The number of in-house counsel is on the increase.

- A gender imbalance still exists, with men outnumbering women. Perhaps one reason for this is that female lawyers take one look at the lifestyle of their male counterparts and are far too smart to sign up to their way of life! However, women are taking on a much more prominent role.

CHANGE AS OPPORTUNITY

It's clear that we're living in times of dramatic professional and social change. Competition, which was once regarded as a dirty word in the profession, is now accepted as an economic fact of life. Competition is increasing, not just within the profession as a result of the growing number of lawyers but also from outside it as a result of deregulation and the move to multi-disciplinary partnerships. Whichever way you look at it, the days of law being considered a vocation are now dead and buried. Law is now a dynamic business.

You may have read the proverbial story of two shoe salesmen sent to Africa 50 years ago. One reported to his office, "All the natives here walk about barefoot and so there is no market," whereas the other reported, "All the natives here walk about barefoot, so there is a tremendous opportunity to sell shoes." Given the same circumstances, one person sees a problem, the other an opportunity.

> *"People are always blaming their circumstances for*
>
> *what they are. I don't believe in circumstances.*
>
> *The people who get on in this world are the people*
>
> *who get up and look for the circumstances they want, and, if*
>
> *they can't find them, make them."*

GEORGE BERNARD SHAW

To see the changes affecting the legal profession as purely a problem or a threat is a defensive reaction. Instead, they can be regarded as opportunities to excel, explore new markets, learn new skills and to develop, rather than conform to existing and self-limiting beliefs upheld by your competitors. For too long, too many lawyers have been trapped in the "follow the leader" mentality. All of a sudden, they are discovering this is not always the wisest strategy, especially as the leader is competing for their business. I believe it is better to develop your own sense of uniqueness. Most firms like to say they are in some way different. The truth is most aren't. Most have similar offices, offer similar standards of client service, write letters the same way, pay their staff similar rates and manage their people the same way. Do not follow the footprints of others because it will only lead you to the crowd: instead, create your own path.

TAKING CONTROL

One area where the dynamic of change has had greatest impact is in the client-lawyer relationship. In the old days, lawyers were in control of the client-lawyer relationship. They would rarely visit clients; clients came to visit them. These days, the reverse is increasingly common. Clients are now calling the shots. They expect their lawyers to come to them. They are the ones who are defining the parameters of the professional relationship, determining what software they want you to use, how they want to be billed, what they are prepared to pay, which suppliers their lawyers should use, and so on. They are starting to control their business. Yet that does not have to be the case.

You are the master of your own destiny, and as such you have the choice to take control over your practice. Perhaps you need to start to think differently about your practice, your business, and the relationships you have with your clients and colleagues if you are to achieve what you want from life.

THE POINT OF LIFE

While the rules of the game may have changed, the point of it really hasn't. The point of life is to be happy and enjoy life as much as possible. Yet many people seem to miss that point and so play a pointless game, focusing on achieving status, recognition or financial abundance. As David Maister writes in *True Professionalism* (Free Press, 1997),

> *"All other goals (money, fame, status, responsibility, achievement) are merely ways of making you happy. They are worthless in themselves."*

What game are you playing? Many firms seem to think the name of the game is all about all about meeting and exceeding financial targets. Inevitably, this is a cause of dissatisfaction among lawyers. Hindi Greenberg writes in *The Lawyer's Career Change Handbook* (Avon Books, 1998):

"This ethical dilemma and resulting tensions—to watch the clock and not to overcharge, yet to bill as many hours as possible, is one of the most common complaints I hear."

While sound financial management is an important exercise in any business, it is not the object of the exercise. Do not put yourself in the position of taking on any old brief simply to meet budget and make money. You will sell yourself short. Let me give you an example:

I was leading a workshop during which a young lawyer told his story about taking on a criminal case in which he had little experience. He went on to say that the client was a bit of a "sleaze" but because he had the money to pay for a lawyer, he took the case. I ask you, who was really the sleaze in this case?

YOUR PURPOSE
While the point of your life is to be happy, your practice should be the vehicle to help bring about that happiness. That means you need to have a road map and start becoming selective about the roads you go down. First, you need to set some personal goals; for example, decide what you want to do with your leisure time, how much time you want to spend at home, how much money you need to help you along the way. Second, you need to set some goals in your business, and to make decisions about the type of work you like, the calibre of clients you want to serve and the type of environment you want to work in. It's important that your personal goals dictate your business goals and not the other way round.

It has been said many times, do what you love and the money will follow. The world of business is not about balance sheets or corporate entities. It is about people. Regrettably, law school doesn't seem to address this issue or equip graduates with the necessary people skills to get ahead. Legal education traditionally focuses on the technical aspect of being a lawyer. Lawyers in Australia, for example, still tend to have a narrow view of their professional development, referring to it as CLE, or Continuing Legal Education. There is comparatively little emphasis placed on education relating to management, marketing and technology or communication skills. Australia is not the only country like this; a similar pattern is evident in most other jurisdictions.

The point is that in these changing times, your technical pre-eminence, while a necessary prerequisite to your success, will not be sufficient to get you to where you want to go in life. It may get you to the starting line, but considering that there are many other lawyers who have the same expertise as you, you need to be different and stand out from the herd. How do you do that?

BEING HUMAN

International sports management celebrity and lawyer Mark McCormack offers a sensible answer in his book *The Terrible Truth About Lawyers* (Morrow, 1987):

> *"It is the human skills that get practical results. Those are the universal skills that a successful lawyer should have in common with a successful businessman, a successful scientist, a successful anyone."*

How you treat people around you, your clients, your potential clients, your colleagues, your referrers, your suppliers and, importantly, yourself is essentially what will set you apart from mediocre lawyers.

A couple of years ago I watched the movie *Patch Adams*. The story is based on the life and philosophy of Dr Hunter Adams, a doctor who uses less conventional means of medicine, notably laughter, to assist in the healing process of his patients. In the film, Adams is seen training in a medical school run by conservative, conventional doctors who suffer from a common syndrome—they are more fascinated by the disease than the patient. In one scene, all the trainee doctors are doing the rounds of the hospital wards with the senior consultant. The consultant stops by one bed and after looking at the clipboard at the end of the patient's bed, starts asking his students questions about the nature of the patient's illness and the possible prognosis. The patient is largely ignored by the consultant and looks alarmed at the discussions taking place about her fragile condition. Without any acknowledgment of the patient, the consultant then asks his students, "Does anyone have any questions?" to which Adams replies, "Yes, I do, what's the patient's name?"

The point is clear: your "bedside manner" is critical; take an interest in your client.

THE ROLE OF MANAGEMENT

Your practice is your business and like any business, it needs managing. Many firms are now supported by management staff, ranging from a practice manager (often an accountant) to multi-disciplinary teams with a wide range of skills and responsibilities including financial management, marketing, client relationships, tenders and proposals, knowledge management, information technology and human resource management.

In order to get ahead, many lawyers have embarked on sophisticated and costly programs designed to make them leading edge. International standardisation programs such as Lexcel and those promoted by the International Organisation for Standardisation (ISO) have undoubtedly brought many internal benefits to legal businesses and helped to shape more businesslike cultures within such organisations. However, there is a risk that too many businesses look to such techniques as panaceas for all their ills. While some of these techniques benefit some legal businesses, many of them do not address the human skills Mark McCormack talks about.

While refining systems and setting the benchmark for client service standards, the impact of some of these programs can nevertheless be constraining on innovation and creativity. Too many rules and regulations can end up ruling and regulating people's behaviour. Perhaps your practice is like this?

David Freemantle, one of Britain's leading writers on management, puts it best in his book *The 80 Things You Must Do to Be a Great Boss* (McGraw-Hill, 1995):

> *"There is no miracle cure for management problems. In fact, there is no new theory of modern management. There never will be and there never has been."*

So, a note of caution. Management does not hold the key to your success—you do. It is not the sole responsibility of your practice manager or financial controller to make you a profit; nor is it the sole responsibility of your marketing manager to attract new business and retain it; nor is it the sole responsibility of your human resources manager to train your people into the professionals you want them to be. You share those responsibilities. By all means let them get on with the job you have hired them for and respect them as the professionals they are, but don't wash your hands of all responsibility for those tasks. You have a vested interest in being a part of their success.

THE FUTURE

What we do know is that the legal profession today is changing rapidly. Nothing seems certain any more. Mergers, takeovers and redundancies are all commonplace in what has become a ruthless business world, the legal business included. To survive in this new environment, firms need to have a culture that is flexible enough to embrace change yet still maintain traditional values. The successful firms will be those that put their people first and the rest—client loyalty, staff commitment, quality of service and profit—will follow.

JAMES O'LOGHLIN

James is a former criminal lawyer who turned to comedy as a career. Today, he is a writer and a television chat show host in Sydney, Australia.

Why did you choose to leave the law?
I had been running parallel careers for a couple of years, criminal law by day, stand-up comedy by night. During my final two years as a lawyer I only worked three days a week, then two, and I was also writing for a radio station. At the beginning of 1999 I realised I had been using the fact that I was still a lawyer as an excuse not to really push the stand-up comedy boat out and see where it might go. When I resigned, I certainly didn't dislike my job, but I wanted to see what would happen if I committed to comedy full time.

Is there a motto that sums up your philosophy to life?
The nearest I get to that is how I motivate myself when I'm scared to try something. I imagine myself in 30 years time, wishing I'd had a bit more guts and lamenting what might have been, and that image is always scarier.

Do you believe lawyers are doing enough to help advance society?
As in any group of people, some are, some aren't. Most people act selfishly. I didn't leave a private law firm and join legal aid because I wanted to help advance society, I did it because I thought I'd enjoy the job. What the law does is provide a large number of well-paid, intellectually stimulating jobs that don't have much social value. Who's to blame? I don't know.

A lot of corporate lawyers don't realise that a job that throws you into the thick of the problems of real people can be far more interesting than one dealing with corporate problems, because it adds a dimension that corporate law often lacks: people.

I would also add that the curriculums of universities and law schools have traditionally virtually ignored the social dimension of the law. For example, it will emphasise the elements of a crime, not its causes and cures. When that aspect of education is ignored, it is perhaps not surprising the practitioners who emerge also ignore it.

How can lawyers change adverse public perception?

It is difficult because people only come to see a lawyer when they have a problem, so they are already in a bad mood. Almost by definition, half the time their problem isn't going to resolve the way they want it to, so they are going to be in a worse mood. And when they get the bill, they'll get even grumpier. But despite this, most lawyers have a fairly healthy relationship with most of their clients. I wouldn't waste time beating yourself up about public perceptions, just concentrate on making sure you're doing a good job for your own clients.

What can the leaders of the legal profession do to lay the foundations for the future?

Remember that all lawyers are in a position of privilege—they're highly educated and earn a higher than average income—and that traditionally one of the socially vital roles of lawyers has been to speak on behalf of the voiceless. So that when a government wants to pass another draconian law curtailing the rights of illegal immigrants or those accused of a crime, no-one hears what those directly affected by those laws say. But they'll listen to a lawyer.

What rewards do you find in your new work that were absent before?

It's more interesting, more frivolous and more diverse, and if I stuff up no-one goes to jail.

What are the secrets of your success?

The hardest part of achieving anything, I think, is working out what you want to achieve. I was lucky in that I stumbled upon comedy and almost immediately felt that I wanted to do it. Once you work out what you want to do, the rest is simple. You just keep doing it. That in itself is success. If someone eventually notices, that's a bonus.

Do you welcome the gradual erosion of the divisions between the professions?

Yes, I see a world where you will be able to go to an accountant who is also a ballerina and a chef and he or she will entertain you with a dazzling rendition of Swan Lake while they do your tax and cook you up a lovely spag bol. To be honest, I have no idea, but I wouldn't want a financial planner doing my bail application.

Are lawyers greedy?

Everyone is greedy. Lawyers sometimes have more opportunity to be greedy than others. Some are, some aren't

Is there one person who has inspired you beyond any others?

I had a client who told me about the most horrific life she had led in a matter-of-fact way—only because I pressed her to—and she didn't allow herself to use any of it as an excuse, even though she would have had every justification in the world for doing so.

What advice would you give someone embarking on a legal career?

There are many, many different types of jobs a lawyer can do, from sitting in an office to standing in court. Think clearly about what interests you: people or companies; writing or talking; crime or the environment. Don't think that if you keep doing a job you hate for a while that eventually you'll be a partner and everything will be wonderful—it's not true. Trust your instincts; if you think you might like Family Law, give it a go. How else are you going to know?

CHAPTER 2

Practising Best Practice

"The marketplace is no respecter of age, race, colour or sex. It rewards ingenuity and service wherever it is found."

JOHN KEYHOE

There are many types of lawyers; men and women of different nationalities all over the world. There are lawyers in private practice, sole practice, government, in-house corporate, the judiciary, education, law enforcement and politics. There are those who are excellent, mediocre, dishonest, extroverted, introverted, happy, sad, married, single, divorced, straight, gay, depressed, alcoholic, conscientious, generous and mean. There are those who have expertise in a variety of areas. It has been predicted that the following practice areas will see big growth over the next decade:

Alternative dispute resolution and mediation
Bankruptcy
Biomedical and bioethical issues
Communications
Computer law
Corporate reorganisation
Criminal law
Employer/employee relations
Environmental law
Government relations and lobbying
Health care
Immigration law
Intellectual property
International law
Pensions
Probate
Science and technology

The legal profession certainly represents a smorgasbord of life and an industry that continues to offer tremendous opportunities. Figures from the Australian Bureau of Statistics suggest that the legal services industry in that country is booming, with law firms' pre-tax profits per partner 43% higher in 1998-99 than in 1995-96. Much of the boom is being attributed to strong growth in many practice areas. However, the picture isn't all rosy.

WORKING TOO HARD FOR TOO LITTLE

Contrary to public opinion, most lawyers are not rich. Whether they are working in the private or public sector, many are working too hard for too little. Indeed, if the figures for NSW in Australia are anything to go by, then life as a lawyer is nothing like as lucrative as the general public might believe. In NSW, 60% of lawyers earn $75,000 or less a year (real take-home after all expenses but before income tax) and just 10% earn above $150,000 a year. Even in the United States, a country with more than a million lawyers and where most of them are perceived to be rich, the median income of attorneys is just $60,000 a year.

Lawyers also suffer from two major problems—having too much work and too much stress.

According to a survey published by the Law Society of NSW in 1999, having too much work is a challenge for more than 50% of practitioners, while 14% claimed that they don't have enough work! Clearly the majority have no problem billing clients. Lawyers in some of the larger firms are billing up to eight hours a day. In some of the major US firms, that figure is higher.

The demanding schedule is obviously taking its toll on lawyers. The survey added: "Women lawyers, lawyers working full time, those working in Community Legal Centres and private practitioners in very large firms were more likely than most to report some form of work-related stress."

This raises a simple issue. Do you want to try to make lots of money and kill yourself in the process? If so, then put this book down now and head off to Hong Kong, Singapore, New York or London, where salaries can indeed be very attractive.

However, if you would like to get some sort of perspective and balance in your life, then read on. To achieve this goal, you must first ask yourself some soul-searching questions:

- Who do I like to work with (and who don't I like to work with)?
- What sort of work fulfils me (and what doesn't)?
- Why don't I have enough time for my family and friends?
- Where would I like to work (in the city? in the country? at home? in a smaller partnership? as in-house counsel?)
- When do I get stressed?
- Why do I get stressed?
- Why do I do what I do?

This exercise requires you to be very honest with yourself. It may help to do this with an independent person in whom you can confide and who can probe you about your answers and help to point you in the right direction. It may be that as a result of your answers, you can consider some of the following options:

1. Look for a new career doing something you enjoy much more
2. Develop expertise in other areas of law so as to increase your value to your clients
3. Leave your large practice for a smaller one
4. Leave private practice and become in-house counsel
5. Leave practice as in-house counsel and join a private practice
6. Change the geographic location of your work
7. Become a sole practitioner
8. Develop other commercial interests beyond the law
9. Decide to work for a better class of client
10. Reduce your workload by working part time or flexitime.

This is not meant to be an exhaustive list and none of these strategies is mutually exclusive. For more options, I recommend Hindi Greenberg's book *The Lawyer's Career Change Handbook* (Avon Books, 1998) and Hilary Mantis's *Alternative Careers For Lawyers* (Random House, 1997). Both are US publications and offer valuable assistance to those considering career change.

WHAT IS IMPORTANT TO YOU?

Earlier, I raised the issue about the point of life—to be happy. As I suggested, your practice is the vehicle to help you attain that objective. So what will make you happy? Money? Health? Achievement? Relationships? Adventure? Maybe it's all of these. Whatever your answer, your work should be an embodiment of what makes you happy. In other words, if the five areas listed above will make you happy, your work must meet all the following criteria:

1. It should be profitable
2. It should allow for a healthy daily regime
3. It should offer you the opportunity to achieve something
4. It should allow time for you to maintain relationships with those most important to you in life
5. It should satisfy your sense of adventure.

Perhaps the most important criterion for most people is money. For most of us, it is like oxygen; when you need it, you need it! To attain many important things in life such as homes, children's education and holidays, you need money. Essentials as well as life's luxuries come with a price tag attached. So the challenge remains, how to build a thriving practice that fulfils you personally and professionally, and yet earns you the freedom that money buys.

WORKING SMARTER NOT HARDER

Many lawyers assume that if they work hard, they will earn this freedom. Some think that burning the midnight oil will impress their superiors and get them ahead in their careers. Yet working hard and being busy without working towards some clearly defined goals is not the smartest strategy to achieve this end. This is a slave strategy. Unless they are complete sycophants or workaholics, they cannot really say they are enjoying what they do. Even if money is their only goal, this is still a foolish strategy. If you work hard in your job, you'll make a living; if you work smarter, you can make a fortune.

Smart lawyers are effective delegators and have enough free time to do the things they enjoy. In contrast, the hard workers are slaving away in the office being martyrs to a cause—one which they often have no stake in!

You can always spot smart workers by these attributes:

1. THEY ARE RECOGNISED AS EXPERTS AT SOMETHING
They appreciate that the more of an expert they are, the fewer competitors they are likely to have and the more they can charge! They understand that the more one offers what everyone else offers, the more one will experience greater price sensitivity among clients.

2. THEY WORK MORE ON THEIR PRACTICE, NOT IN IT
They take time out from their busy schedule to think about ways to work on their business, not just in it. They strive to find new ways to work more efficiently and effectively.

3. THEY HAVE A SENSE OF PURPOSE
This is their personal strategy, or road map for their success. They don't set themselves self-limiting goals. They think about who they are and where they are going.

4. THEY STRIVE TO BE EXCELLENT IN ALL THEY DO

They recognise that if they are not getting better at what they do, then in real terms they are getting worse. Their value on the market will decrease if they do not strive for excellence in all that they do. They ask themselves, "What is one skill that if I did it excellently would have the biggest impact on my career?"

5. THEY LEAVE CLIENTS BETTER OFF THAN WHEN THEY MET THEM

Their job is only successfully completed when the client's position is improved thanks to their input, not when they have billed the client and closed the file! That is their value, not the hours that they put in.

6. THEY LEARN TO SAY NO

They cannot be all things to all men. They learn to abandon the low end of the market and to free themselves up to serve the higher end. They know there will be plenty of people who will look after the low end!

7. THEY ARE ACTION ORIENTATED

Lots of people in business live in a dream world; these people don't. They fulfil their hopes and aspirations because they take action.

8. THEY STAY IN GREAT S.H.A.P.E.

They have:

Skills: They keep learning and so keep getting better at what they do.

Health: They stay on top of it. Good diet and regular exercise promote good health, which gives them the energy they need to stay ahead and achieve their goals.

Attitude: Henry Ford once said, "If you think you can do a thing or think you can't do a thing, you are right." Smart people think they can. They focus

on the positive, not the negative, and look for solutions rather than focus on the problems.

Persistence: In spite of occasional setbacks, they don't give up. Whenever I find myself feeling low, I think about one man who never gives up—the internationally renowned speaker W. Mitchell. His persistence is inspirational. Mitchell has suffered two major setbacks in his life: one was a motorcycle accident which left him with burns to over 60% of his body, the other was a plane crash which left him a paraplegic. In spite of his terrible injuries, he has made something special out of his life and these days he inspires thousands of people around the world with his simple yet profound message: "It's not what happens to you, it's what you do about it that counts."

Enthusiasm: The word "enthusiasm" stems from the Greek "en theo", which means "inner God". As the American philosopher Ralph Waldo Emerson once said, "Nothing great was ever achieved without enthusiasm."

What you believe and what you value determines how you act on a daily basis. If you are to change how you act, you need to examine your beliefs and your philosophy about your work. It all starts with you. Taking the time to consider who you are and what you want to become is essential to getting to the top end of your profession. As in all professions, when you get to the top the view is pretty good. To get there, the key is to work smarter, not harder.

Traditionally, lawyers considered they had "arrived" when they received an invitation to partnership. While undoubtedly there are privileges and benefits to being a partner, there are also heavy responsibilities. The status of being a partner today is not what it used to be 20 years ago. The important thing is to set your goals bigger than just achieving partnership and to look at new ways of doing things.

I once listened to an address by Jay Abraham, one of America's top marketing gurus, at a symposium in Los Angeles. He made this important point:

"Don't limit your vision of yourself or your business."

Abraham pointed out that too many people "draw a line in the sand" beyond which they or their businesses never progress. When they limit their strategy and vision, they don't ever fulfil their true potential. As a result, they effectively steal from potential clients who are deprived of the opportunity to use innovative services and ultimately they are stealing from themselves.

Look beyond the norms in your industry and try to find new ways of doing things that will help your clients and customers and set you apart from your competitors.

Don't be too influenced by what your peers might think about your plans. What your clients think is far more important. They are the ones who present the opportunities and keep your career and your business alive. If you settle for safety, security and second-best, your work will become tedious and tiresome. Avoid holding on to work that could be delegated, and get out of the trap of doing it yourself because it keeps your budget healthy. This widespread practice is, in fact, unhealthy and inefficient: unhealthy because you risk going into a complacent cruise mode and depriving younger lawyers of the opportunity to grow; inefficient because you are working on matters that could be carried out by someone less experienced while you're charging the client for your time.

Many lawyers and law firms have not yet come to terms with this way of thinking; their misguided response to competition has been to compete on price by discounting.

Unless you are operating in a commodity type of market such as conveyancing, this kind of response can rarely be justified. After all, people value something by what they pay for it; the more they pay, the better they think it must be (and should be!), provided you give them a reason to pay and you deliver on what you promise.

The English philosopher John Ruskin cautioned people nearly 150 years ago about the dangers of paying too little for something of value:

"It's unwise to pay too much, but it's worse to pay too little. When you pay too much, you lose a little money, that's all. When you pay too little, you sometimes lose everything because the product you bought was incapable of doing the things it was bought to do. The common law of business practice prohibits paying a little and getting a lot... it can't be done. If you deal with the lowest bidder it is well to add something for the risk you run, and if you do that, you'll have enough to pay for something better."

Practising best practice is about understanding your value, working on what you are worth, delivering value, and charging for it! Once you do that, you will be well on your way to becoming a superstar lawyer.

ROSS HOLMES

Ross is the director of Ross Holmes Limited, a boutique company based in New Zealand that specialises in business, asset protection, trusts and taxation. He is also the founder of Ross Holmes Lawyers, a boutique law firm specialising in commercial and property law.

Why did you choose law as a career?

I stumbled into it after a family friend, a QC in Wellington, suggested it might be an appropriate career move for me. At the time, I had no idea about law. After entering the profession, I went into partnership in 1975. I then went solo in 1986 and now I employ 25 or so people. We are still small and always will be. The practice started as a boutique tax practice. Then I went from being a tax practitioner with limited conveyancing experience to developing a property law expertise with the aim of developing an estate planning practice. Changes in society have promoted needs that didn't exist before.

Is there a motto that sums up your philosophy about life?

If you fail to plan, you plan to fail.

What can the leaders of the legal profession do to lay the foundations for the future?

Offer services to the profession that are of use to it rather than publicising the prosecution of the undesirable element. Currently, lawyers are perceived as ambulances at the bottom of the cliff. They are not performing services designed to enhance the performance and profitability of members of the profession.

Small and medium-sized firms have little or no experience in management systems, bulk purchasing and overhead minimisation. While there are educational seminars available, no emphasis is placed on taking specialist work or referring specialist work to a specialist as a method of enhancing business as opposed to losing it.

The legal profession is the only one that thinks it can walk on water. It is not fostering a co-operative network of lawyers. In New Zealand, there is no useful website that offers referrals to lawyers under their areas of specialty. People like me are perceived as a threat. I advertise on my own. The profession has no idea about marketing; they see it as stealing clients. It is a Dark Age mentality. Some see law as a profession; I see it as a business. It is difficult to change attitudes.

What rewards do you find in your business?
The ability to achieve real results for my clients that help them achieve their overall objectives more safely. Doing our work well and following up with our clients is something that generates satisfied clients and referred business from their children and friends. Most people who sell trusts and who don't follow up have clients who see their lawyers as an evil necessity and therefore don't recommend them to others.

What do you do to make your clients feel special?
If I did a trust for a client without him relating to it as a worthwhile exercise, then I wouldn't achieve half of what I do achieve. It is important to make clients understand the benefits. I like my clients to attend my seminars first to understand what we can offer them. Then at each meeting we focus on their objectives before attempting to sell any service to them, thereby developing empathy with them.

Do you welcome the gradual erosion of the divisions between the professions?
Yes, it is essential unless you can have a one-stop shop and it's almost impossible to do so, because of the nature of being self-employed. I have had discussions with other businesses about combined marketing. This tends not to work because they concentrate on their own businesses. The accounting firms who offer the one-stop shop under their own roof could succeed.

What are the secrets of your success?
Common sense. All we are doing is simplifying the complex. In our case, trusts are regarded as alien by clients. They are legal devices that they cannot understand. We tell people about basic trust concepts and we give people practical advice and draft minutes that will be brilliant and will stand challenge.

Are lawyers greedy?
I don't know. At the end of the day it is the quality of the result that matters. If the focus is to provide a narrow range of services, then the result for the client will be narrow. This creates a perception of lawyers' fees being

too high. In my website, I promote the idea that experts of necessity are more expensive than general practitioners. A one-off fee will save a heap of money if the longer term benefits are offered.

What advice would you offer someone embarking on a legal career?
First, obtain as broad a range of experience as possible before determining which field you want to be involved in. As part of your degree, make sure you obtain brilliant computer skills and very good accounting knowledge as well as marketing and business skills.

CHAPTER 3

Connecting with Existing Clients

"A special product might make you competitive.
Differentiated services may make you distinct.
But only carefully crafted relationships will create
a breakthrough firm."

ALAN WEISS

In 1992, I watched a television interview with the late Professor Fred Hollows. He was a New Zealand-born ophthalmologist who gave thousands of people, all over the world, their eyesight back. In particular, he launched a national program to attack eye disease in Australian Aborigines. He went on to make a difference in the lives of many by introducing simple surgical techniques to communities that couldn't afford mainstream ophthalmic care, especially those in the Aboriginal communities. I will always remember him saying that his purpose in life was "to serve".

Fred Hollows had no trouble connecting with his clients. He was clear about his purpose and his passion for his work earned him the recognition he deserved.

Lawyers can learn from Fred Hollows's example. If they spent less time thinking about meeting budget and more time thinking about how they can assist others, then their world and the world around them would be far better places. Helping people get what they want is the best way to help you get what you want. That should be the motivation behind every business relationship you have with a client.

WHAT'S THIS ABOUT SELLING?

As a criminal lawyer I was never taught to sell. The police were my salespeople, providing a steady stream of business for my practice. Even those lawyers who are practising in the lucrative areas of commercial and financial work are not taught to sell. Yet by definition, every lawyer needs to be a salesperson. Nevertheless, the mere mention of the word "sell" makes most lawyers cringe. They tend not to regard themselves as salespeople as they associate the word "selling" with people who sell products or services that they don't believe in, or whose sole motivation is to take your order and make you part with your money. (Cynics might argue that this description could apply to quite a few lawyers anyway!)

So what is the lowdown on selling? Here are some insights that should make you less sensitive to the idea of selling.

Keith Abraham explains in his book *Creating Loyal Profitable Customers* (People Pursuing a Passion, 1999), that there are two types of salespeople:

First, there are "product pushers", who have the following characteristics:

- They do not build relationships with customers or clients
- There is little rapport between buyer and seller
- Their integrity and credibility is in question.

In contrast, there are the other type of salespeople, the "solutions providers". These people demonstrate the following attributes:

- They do build relationships with customers or clients
- They do have an interest in helping their customers or clients achieve their objectives
- They improve themselves continually so that the client considers their expertise an asset
- They have integrity and credibility
- They don't just tell clients what the product or service is (e.g. "I do estate planning"), they show them what it will do for them (e.g. "I can help you to retire rich").

Clearly, lawyers come within the second category. They are solutions providers.

Selling in the context of the legal industry is not about closing techniques or sales scripts. However, your ability to listen to and understand the concerns of a client is an essential part of communicating and building rapport. The type of sales courses that work towards that objective are very worthwhile.

Keith Abraham points out that the easiest thing to do is to sell something once; your challenge is to have your clients keep coming back time and time again. I wonder how many files you have in your office of clients who used your service once and never returned? Have you wondered why they didn't come back and use you again?

American research has suggested that 68% of clients shop around and take their business elsewhere because of an attitude of "indifference" to the client on the part of the adviser. In other words, clients don't feel that they or their business is valued.

Other reasons cited are:

> Dissatisfaction with the outcome or service (14%)
> Price (9%)
> Other relationships (5%)
> Client relocation (3%).

Note the relative insignificance of price. Perhaps many firms create indifferent clients because they are still too busy chasing new clients rather than looking after existing ones. Recent research in Britain suggests that up to one-third of firms do not even know how much of their new business comes from existing clients!

How can you prevent your clients falling into a state of indifference?

UNDERSTAND THE 80/20 RULE
Most people who have been in business for more than 10 minutes or so have probably had the 80/20 rule drummed into their heads. (If it's any consolation to those who don't know about the 80/20 rule, I have to admit I had never heard of it until I was completing post-graduate studies. They just didn't cover this stuff when I was at law school!)

The 80/20 rule is also known as Pareto's Principle. Vilfredo Pareto was a 19th-century Italian economist who found that 80% of production volume came from only 20% of the producers. Taking this philosophy further, it means that 80% of your income comes from 20% of your clients, 80% of your office problems come from 20% of your employees, and 80% of your headaches come from 20% of your clients! Some people in business question this rule as it applies less to some businesses than to others. Some law firms I have worked with find 60/40 to be nearer the mark.

The point is that you will have clients who appreciate you and your service more than other clients and who will stick with you through thick and thin. They are a good source of referral, are consistently more profitable, pay their bills promptly and are more enjoyable to work with than others. These clients are the ones who are the mainstay behind your business and these are the ones to whom you should be devoting your time. Let's call them "A" clients.

Most firms generally devote about 60% of their efforts to generating new business from existing clients, including their A clients.

It is a good idea to categorise your clients on your database (if you haven't got one, don't panic, read on) and to classify them as follows:

"A" clients—clients described above
"B" clients—those with long-term potential to be A clients
"C" clients—one-off clients
"D" clients—clients who waste your time.

Assuming you have a body of A or B clients, you are better off building the relationship with them first before spending your time, money and energy trying to "upgrade" a C or D client. It's also potentially more productive than spending time chasing a new client who is probably well looked after by another lawyer anyway.

It is a lot less expensive getting new work from existing clients than getting new business from new clients. Principally, this is because you have established a relationship with a client who trusts you and has confidence in you. So make sure you capture the opportunities with your existing A and B clients before working out how to get new clients.

CREATING EMOTIONAL VALUE

Alan Weiss, author of *Million Dollar Consulting* (McGraw-Hill, 1992, 1998), suggests the key to success in a consulting type business is to craft relationships with clients.

The Macquarie Dictionary defines "relationship" as "an emotional connection between people, sometimes involving sexual relations". I don't intend to offer insights into how to achieve the second half of this definition! As in any business, there is a clear line to be drawn between a business and a personal relationship. While it is perfectly possible and proper to connect at an emotional level with a client ("I like working with this person"), a little caution is needed when it comes to "loving your clients to death".

In his book *The Justice Game* (Vintage, 1999), Geoffrey Robertson QC gives a succinct reminder to lawyers about such an approach:

"Love, in law as in life, gets in the way of sound judgment—it leads to tactical errors, to over-emotional arguments and most dangerously, to lies."

However, the importance of making an emotional connection with your prospects and clients needs to be emphasised. Leading English writer David Freemantle, author of *What Customers Like About You* (Nicholas Brealy, 1998), says:

"Where there is no emotional value in a relationship, there is effectively no relationship, at best an incidental and momentary interaction as a customer undertakes a transaction and walks way... those companies that are consistently successful in business excel at adding emotional value to virtually everything they do."

Perhaps the legal profession's desire to give independent, impartial and sound advice has led to accusations of its members being aloof, arrogant and uncaring. While understanding the boundary between getting too close to a client and creating an emotional connection is a start, there is still a great deal that lawyers can do to create a more positive perception about their service and value within society.

Outlined below and in successive chapters are more than 100 ideas that can help you do this and give you greater job satisfaction in the process. The ideas in this chapter focus on building stronger relationships with your existing clients.

IDEA #1
BE CLEAR ABOUT THE VALUE YOU BRING TO YOUR CLIENTS

Many lawyers, indeed many people in business, have little appreciation of the value of the work they do beyond the actual task that they carry out. They tend to focus on the features of their service rather than on the benefits or the value to the client. Just pick up any law firm brochure or run your eyes over their Yellow Pages advertisements and you will see what I mean. This is a really critical issue. Put yourself in a customer or client's shoes for a moment and imagine what it would be like firstly to buy a car and secondly to be one of your own clients.

When you consider buying a car, you can admire it in a number of ways; you can feel the comfort of the seats, smell the leather interior and take the vehicle for a test drive. The car has a fixed price tag. If the car breaks down in any way, it is obvious to you: the engine won't start, the fuel pump breaks down or the stereo malfunctions. In such a case, you rarely take it personally as the car is manufactured in a factory. The car can be warranted to cover failures such as these and that gives you protection and confidence when you buy.

In contrast, when you consider turning to a lawyer for advice, you cannot sense much about the service. You cannot "feel" the advice, "smell" the lawyer, or even take him for a test drive. In most cases, his service doesn't have a price tag beyond an hourly rate. Knowing when the lawyer's advice is bad is often impossible for you to detect. If the lawyer fails to deliver on his promise, then, in contrast to the car breakdown, you are more likely to take it personally. As most services come without a warranty or a guarantee, you tend to be uncertain and fearful about the value of the service you are buying.

While there are differences between buying the car and legal advice, there is one notable similarity: both types of customer are buying emotional outcomes. The customer who buys a car is buying peace of mind, knowing that the service offered with the car includes after-sales support, on-going service, maintenance and safety. The car itself is simply a commodity that gets the manufacturer onto the starting line in a fiercely competitive industry.

Similarly, clients of a legal practice are also buying peace of mind, knowing that their problem is safe in their lawyer's hands and that he can provide the solution they are looking for. The lawyer's expertise, experience and time are simply the commodities which gets him onto the starting line.

Defining the emotional outcome of your service for your client is therefore crucial to your marketing success. This is a simple concept to grasp and yet surprisingly few lawyers apply it in practice.

Perhaps the emotional outcome for a client of a divorce lawyer might be "I want to start a new life", and for a customer using an estate planning lawyer it might be "I want to avoid the taxman and retire rich". Once you can define your client's emotional outcome, then you have a much more compelling proposition to make to your prospects. An additional spin-off is that you can establish your fees accordingly, rather than charging by the hour for every assignment. You will be much clearer and more confident about what you really do for a living and consequently people will take much more notice of you. They will remember you.

IDEA #2

MAKE SURE YOUR COLLEAGUES UNDERSTAND THE VALUE OF YOUR WORK

I'm often amazed at the number of people working in legal practices who seem to know surprisingly little about the work that their colleagues do. All your colleagues should be able to state clearly what you do for your clients and be able to promote you when the occasion arises.

Your receptionist or "director of first impressions" needs to be particularly aware of who does what around the office so that he or she can field calls knowledgeably and effectively. I recall going into a law office in Wellington, New Zealand, for a meeting with one of the partners. After introducing myself to the receptionist, it was clear she had no idea in what areas of the law the firm operated, let alone what value this individual partner contributed to his clients.

As a test, try asking your secretary, personal assistant and your "director of first impressions" how they would describe what you do. If they don't have the right answer, put them right! If they don't know what you do, how can you expect your prospects and clients to know?

IDEA #3

STORE ALL CONTACT INFORMATION ON YOUR DATABASE

If you haven't got one already (and many lawyers don't), start compiling a database that enables you to store important information about your clients, suppliers, referrers and other important contacts. As a minimum, you need to capture the following information:

- Full contact details
- How they heard about you
- People they have referred you to
- Personal assistant's name
- Client classification listing (A, B or C)
- Relevant family details
- Client case history

While most firms have some form of marketing database, a well-maintained and well-managed database is a rarity. However, they are crucial to your marketing and relationship management. In Britain, the trend seems to be towards using package databases. (Just over 60% of those with a central marketing database favour them.) They not only act as a database, but also enable recording of client information and can assist with transmission of faxes and emails as well as transcription of documents directly from the desktop. Microsoft's Access, Lawbase, ACT and Tracker are some well-known brand names.

The remainder use bespoke systems; in other words, database applications that have been written for their particular needs.

Packaged databases tend to be more popular because they are easier to upgrade and interface with other office applications

IDEA #4
FORM A CLIENT ADVISORY BOARD

This is a powerful idea and one I have used in my business to good effect. Sometimes lawyers are faced with difficult management or operational decisions. Because of their powerful intellects, lawyers have a habit of thinking they know it all and so make (often ill-informed) decisions all on their own. If this sounds like you, let go of your ego and let someone else help you for a change!

A cost-effective way of doing this is to establish a client advisory board. You can either arrange this at a firm level, or just for yourself. What you do is to invite half a dozen good clients/referrers to sit on your client advisory board. The purpose is to get their advice and opinions about your practice. They may have faced similar dilemmas in their businesses and so this forum becomes useful for the exchange of helpful information. In the process, you also create a potentially valuable network by introducing clients who may not have met each other before.

When I formed my board, I hand-picked people who I knew had good networks, whom I trusted, and who had experience in business that often far exceeded mine. I briefed each of them about the challenges I faced in my business and invited them to a meeting after work in a quiet corner in the bar of a 5-star hotel. After drinks and open discussion, I took them out to dinner at my expense as my way of saying thank you. This is not difficult to do and people genuinely appreciate being invited to play a part in your success.

IDEA #5
HOLD A SCENARIO SEMINAR

If you are looking to get your clients to use your firm more often (i.e. cross sell), then try this excellent idea that I learnt from Australian marketing expert Winston Marsh. It is particularly appropriate if your firm offers a range of services and you are trying to inform your clients about them and to engage your firm more often.

Here's what you can do:
Invite a group of suitable clients to a free function which is promoted as 60 minutes of information and fun. Aim to have no more than 50 people there. The event could be staged after work at your office.

Call the event something along the lines of "How to Avoid the Week from Hell—Everything You Need to Know from Six of Our Best!"

Invite them to bring two friends. Identify six areas of practice and get six of your lawyers to present for 10 minutes each. Each presentation follows on from the other and tells a story about a hypothetical client. As an example, let's consider a married, 50-year-old male self-employed property developer.

The event might run in this sequence:
Presenter 1 (your expert in motoring offences)
What happens if you drink too much this evening and you are stopped at the roadside? What are your rights, what are the penalties, what will happen to you if you are caught?

Presenter 2 (your expert in family law)
What happens when you get home from the police station and your life partner/spouse has your bags packed and asks you to leave the matrimonial home?

Presenter 3 (your expert in intellectual property law)
Your week gets worse! What happens when you go back to work and you discover your secretary has resigned to join a competitor, taking with her intellectual property belonging to your business?

Presenter 4 (your expert in employment law)
The next day, an employee's fixed term contract expires. What do you do if the employee turns up for work after the expiry date?

Presenter 5 (your expert in property development law)
What if later in the week you receive a letter from the local council informing you that the condominium development does not have appropriate resource or planning consents?

Presenter 6 (your expert in estate planning)
You discover that your eldest son, the beneficiary in a discretionary trust, has become a heroin addict. To finish off an appalling week, you are involved in a road accident and as a result of head injuries, you will be unable to return to work indefinitely. You have made no will, and have no enduring power of attorney! What do you do?

Each presenter in the 10 minutes allocated gives the nuts and bolts of what every client ought to know in each scenario. It is a fun event for clients and staff and certainly beats those boring cocktail functions. It has two added bonuses: first, it forces each of the participants to make a good presentation, an essential skill in the legal business, and second, an event like this helps to promote an integrated, unified partnership.

IDEA #6
GET OUT OF YOUR OFFICE AND GO VISIT YOUR CLIENTS
I share my office with an accountant, Bob McInnes. He is different from many accountants in that he spends much of his time out of the office. He appreciates that clients prefer him to look over their affairs at their home, farm, factory, office or warehouse rather then them having to make the effort to visit him at his office. In doing so he is better equipped to develop an understanding of each client's business. This generates new business directly from those clients who also refer their contacts to him. They like the way he does business. Your clients will like it if you do this, too. I have interviewed hundreds of clients of law firms and patent attorneys in countries as diverse as New Zealand, Australia, America, England, France, Switzerland and Germany. No client has ever complained about his or her lawyer or professional adviser coming to visit. The opposite tends to be true. Here's what one client I interviewed said to me:

CONTINUED ON PAGE 54

CARMEN ARGIBAY

Carmen is a Criminal Judge in Buenos Aires, Argentina and President of the International Federation of Women Judges, Washington D.C., USA

Is there a motto that sums up your philosophy about life?
I don't have one but several. One of my favourites is "What you do with sincerity pays the greatest reward". Another is "Good humour is the best companion".

Do you believe lawyers are doing enough to help advance society?
No, I don't. I am not fond of generalising but I think they have lost the concept that every profession must be a service to society.

What would you suggest lawyers do to overcome adverse public perception?
Adverse public perception generally has its roots in what we do wrong. We must look candidly at our mistakes and try to mend them. Doing it, not just talking about it, will change the perception for the best.

What can the leaders of the legal profession do to lay the foundations for the future?
They can revitalise moral principles that have become somewhat dormant: honesty, hard work, ethics, generosity and commitment.

What rewards do you find in your work?
My best reward is my peace of mind and conscience after delivering a special or difficult judgment, even if I am exhausted.

Do lawyers do enough to make a difference in society?
I think not, we should try harder.

What are the secrets of your success?
Faithfulness to my moral principles, hard work, dedication, an easy way of laughing at myself and the ability to listen to others.

Do you welcome the gradual erosion of the divisions between the professions?
No, I don't. I don't believe one person can know about everything; I think divisions allow us to specialise in what suits us best in terms of intelligence, sentiments, etc. That means we can do better work, even if it's on a restricted field.

Are lawyers greedy?
Some are, some aren't. It is unfair to generalise because it has nothing to do with the profession but with the personality.

Is there any one person who has inspired you beyond any other?
Yes, but you probably have never heard of her. She was a medical doctor and a socialist politician in Argentina whose name was Alicia Moreau de Justo. She lived to be 100 years old and I met her when she was more or less 90. Of course, there are others, particularly my mother.

What advice would you give someone embarking on a legal career?
To anyone starting a career, legal or not, I would advise them to be true to her or his conception of life, and to try and help others because that is the best way to help oneself.

CONTINUED FROM PAGE 51

"We don't know each other very well and this doesn't help with communications. In fact, we have never met one of their lawyers even though he has done work for us. They have never been to our offices to see us and a meeting here would certainly help to pull down those barriers a bit. We recognise that lawyers are busy people but we think the legal profession needs to pull down its facade. We step into their expensive building and immediately we are conscious that we are paying for it."

Your presence at a client's place of business shows you are interested in them. It will help you gain a clearer understanding of the business they are in and who their people are. Remember, people don't care how much you know until you show them how much you care.

IDEA #7
SURVEY YOUR CLIENTS AND ASK THEM FOR THEIR FEEDBACK

It is surprising how much resistance there still is on this issue. Recent statistics suggest that just 36% of law firms in England measure client satisfaction for major clients and only 7% do it for all clients. Many of the law firms I have consulted with admit to having spent reasonable sums of money on sometimes unproductive marketing exercises without first asking clients some basic questions. This a bit like a doctor prescribing a drug for an illness that hasn't yet been diagnosed. For a group of supposedly smart professionals, that doesn't seem to be particularly smart thinking.

I regularly meet practice managers and managing partners who admit that their firm has yet to do this exercise because of other "internal priorities". That is a pretty lame excuse. I wonder whether the real reason is a fear of confronting some truths about the standards of service the firm dishes out! After all, people are naturally anxious about hearing something they may not like. If this is your reaction, I urge you to have broad shoulders and to think positively about the exercise rather than focusing only on potentially negative feedback. Good lawyers, like good business people, should always insist on hearing the bad news.

Measurement of existing client satisfaction levels is probably the single most effective marketing tool a firm could employ and yet firms spend, on average, just 7% of their marketing budget on this activity. In many firms, that budget is pitifully small; on average, less than 3% of revenue.

Without finding out what your clients think of you and your service, you will have no accurate idea of what they want. You risk making client relationship or marketing decisions based solely on intuition rather than on fact. By asking your clients, you

- Show you have an interest in them (and in their business)
- Identify where you over-perform or under-perform
- Discover how your service rates in comparison with other firms
- Pinpoint opportunities for new business
- Increase awareness within your firm of the importance of quality service.

Generally, I have found clients to be more than happy to participate in such a survey. The following genuine comments are typical of clients' reactions to participation:

"I am happy to participate as I think it is a good thing and hopefully it will be of benefit to me as a result of whatever improvements they make."

"We are very pleased with the state of our relationship with them and appreciate the opportunity to express some feedback on their performance."

"I commend them for having the courage to expose themselves. I was really pleased when they asked me if I would take part in this survey."

Only in rare instances have I experienced clients declining an invitation and often it is simply due to other commitments. Obviously, the object of the exercise is to obtain candid comments; sometimes, clients tend to be a little less candid if they have a personal criticism of the lawyer they might be dealing with. That's why an independent facilitator can be very useful in eliciting feedback.

How do you go about getting feedback? The next three ideas offer you options:

IDEA #8

FORM A "HOW ARE WE DOING?" GROUP

This is the easiest and most cost-effective method. Invite several small groups (up to eight clients per group) to participate in a "how are we doing?" discussion.

Invite an independent person, possibly a client, but certainly someone capable of asking the questions, to chair a discussion in your boardroom. When inviting your selected clients, you need to call them and ask if they would be prepared to come to your office, preferably late in the day for no more than 90 minutes, to participate in a discussion about what they like, what they don't like, what they need and what they don't need from you and your practice.

When they arrive, greet them yourself and then disappear, leaving them in the capable hands of your chairperson. The meeting preferably should be taped (with the consent of all participants). Otherwise, there should be a scribe to take notes.

The sort of questions you should ask are: "From your point of view ...

- What would we need to do to be the best law practice in our field?
- What aspects of our service could be improved?
- What do you like or dislike about dealing with our firm?
- In what ways could we be of more value to you?
- Is there anything specific we could do to build a stronger relationship with you?
- Compared with other firms you may have used, how do we rate?
- Is there anything you dislike about our service or our people that would deter you from using us more frequently?"

You may find that their answers are very different to what you had imagined they might be!

When the discussions have been completed, listen to the tape (if it was taped) and really take on board their comments. Write to each of the participants, thank them and perhaps send them a small gift as a token of your appreciation. Then take action!

IDEA #9
CARRY OUT A FACE-TO-FACE SURVEY

This is the most expensive but the most effective method. This involves carrying out face-to-face interviews with your clients and representatives from corporate clients—both the decision-makers and those who interact at an operational level with your business.

This is the 5-step process I have used to facilitate this process with my clients:

Step 1: Client selection
Select a group of clients you wish to interview (and not just the ones you know will say complimentary things about you!).

Step 2: Appointment of an interviewer
Appoint an independent person to interview your clients face-to-face. This person should be a good communicator and a skilled interviewer with a sound knowledge of business practice and an awareness of the type of legal issues that are likely to be discussed.

It is helpful to obtain a balance of qualitative information (words and feelings) as well as quantitative information (numbers) about the quality of your service. Such a project could be managed in-house so long as the person carrying out the survey has the full support of the partnership and is seen by the client to be independent of the issues under discussion. Consequently, an independent partner, your practice manager or marketing manager might be suitable choices for this task.

Step 3: Invitation
Send out a letter of invitation such as that contained in the appendices (page 130). It has three pages: the letter, the fax-back form and lastly the questionnaire to be completed in advance of the interview. You will need to follow up, as some clients will not respond. Not because they don't want to participate but simply because your letter disappeared to the bottom of their correspondence file. If you do follow up these invitations you should be able to secure the participation of more than 80% of your invitees.

Step 4: Briefing
Brief the interviewer about the background of each client relationship—the amount they spend, the type of business they are in, the nature of their legal

problems, and so on, so the interviewer is prepared. Before the interview date, the interviewer should try to obtain a completed questionnaire from the client so as to direct him or her to issues that may be of concern.

Step 5: The interview
I suggest that the interviews be carried out without using a tape recorder, as my experience is that it can have an inhibiting effect on interviewees. The questions should be of a similar nature to those used in the "how are we doing" groups. Make sure that the interviewer takes full notes. Each interviewee should be advised that notes of their interview will be taken and appended verbatim to the final report. Make sure that clients agree to this course of action. Some clients occasionally raise issues which they prefer to remain "off the record". Often, the issue they raise is the very issue the interview is trying to uncover. My practice is to explain that to clients and to encourage them to speak freely and on the record. If clients are still uneasy, then I ask if they would be happy for me to include their comments in an unattributable comments section in the report. Generally, clients are happy with this so long as it doesn't reveal their identity. However, you should stress to them that this is an exercise in openness and that the value is in the candour of each participant's response.

Step 6: The results
Finally, the interviewer's job is to do the hard bit—sift through the questionnaires and interviews and distil the salient points.

If a client raises specific concerns, act on them swiftly; otherwise the whole exercise could be counter-productive. Importantly, thank them again for their contribution and if any major changes arise as a result of their input, give them a call; even better, inform all your clients of the results through your newsletter, if you have one.

IDEA #10
PUT PING PONG BALLS IN YOUR RECEPTION AREA
I like this idea because it is so simple and costs you virtually nothing! I saw this at the Novotel Hotel on Collins Street in Melbourne, Australia. It's a clean, comfortable, centrally located hotel that has always looked after me well. At the checkout desk, they used to have a big glass bowl and alongside the bowl, two wire baskets, one filled with pink ping-pong balls, the other with white ping-pong balls. There was a sign inviting guests to place a pink

ball in the glass bowl if they had enjoyed staying at the hotel or a white one if they had not. And guess what? The bowl was full of (mostly) pink balls. Why not try something similar in your office?

It may be different but it's a powerful, visual indicator of what your clients think about you and your service. (If you find yourself having to sneak into the office at 3am to pull out the white balls, you know you have a problem!)

IDEA #11
COMMISSION SOME RESEARCH

In your efforts to practise best practice and to develop your specialty, you need to create the perception that you are indeed the expert in your chosen field. One way to achieve this rapidly is to commission some research that would be of interest to your clients or the niche in which you are trying to get established.

Consider what are some of the burning issues to which some of your clients and prospects would like answers? For example, if you want to gain a reputation as an expert in employment law, hire a researcher to do a study into redundancy trends and issues. Publish a report and send copies to the appropriate media and targeted clients and prospects. A cost-effective way to do this is to approach your local university. Often, their students, especially those studying for a Masters degree or a Ph.D, are looking for projects to carry out as part of their studies and generally they do a great job and charge much less than a market research company.

IDEA #12
PRODUCE A REGULAR NEWSLETTER

Many firms produce newsletters. The drawback with many of them is that they are boring and say little of real value to the reader. Some firms even take the cheap option and send out newsletters that are in fact written and produced by a central body and then sold onto those firms with each firm's name printed on the front to make it look as if it is produced in-house. In my experience, the information tends to focus on recent developments in the law and contains little in the way of interesting information for the reader. As a marketing exercise, its value is questionable because other firms who buy into this scheme are producing exactly the same information. There is little point of difference.

A good newsletter will include the following:

1. Facts and advice
2. A summary of successful cases you have handled
3. Dates of future client seminars and retreats
4. Contact information, including a website address
5. Answers to questions from readers
6. Stories about clients or referrers
7. Articles written by or about clients or referrers
8. Cartoons and photographs
9. Depending on the size of your print run, offer (and charge for) advertising space to clients, referrers and suppliers in your network.
10. An invitation to add a friend or family colleague to the mailing list.

Don't fall into the trap of writing sterile articles about the law. They might interest you but they bore the pants off most readers. It is a false economy to try to do all this yourself. Outsource it to people who are used to editing, typesetting and printing this type of publication. I suggest you employ an editor to project-manage the production of your newsletter.

IDEA #13

PRODUCE YOUR NEWSLETTER ON AUDIO CASSETTE OR COMPACT DISC

Why not be different and develop an audio newsletter? Depending on your time commitments, you could do this monthly, quarterly or just three times a year. The format for this can be very similar in content to the newsletter I discussed earlier. The only difference is that your thoughts and those of your interviewees are on audio tape. If you are not confident about fronting it, approach your local radio station and ask if one of their well-known broadcasters will do this for you. You may find the radio station will also help you with production. If the information is interesting and valuable, then you may even want to consider selling it to subscribers. Audio tapes are great for business people to listen to in their cars. I have discovered other industries that use this technique, but have yet to find a lawyer. Here's your opportunity. (You could even record your "Week From Hell" seminar and distribute it to all your clients and prospects.)

IDEA #14

ASK, "HAVE YOU THOUGHT ABOUT DOING IT THIS WAY?"

Most clients welcome you asking this question and bringing them fresh ideas. However, don't assume that because your firm offers another service that the client needs, that the client will automatically choose your firm to act on that matter as well. This is particularly true where a colleague is offering the additional service. In such circumstances, a new relationship has to be built.

Once, while conducting a client survey, I interviewed a female client who was using the firm for conveyancing matters. She told me that during a meeting with her legal adviser, she let it be known that she was suffering marriage problems. Apparently, the conveyancing lawyer enthusiastically hauled her down the corridor to introduce her to the firm's family lawyer, whom she had never met before. Her comments are instructive:

> *"I did know of other solicitors in the matrimonial field at that time but I am not particularly assertive and would have liked to have had some time to think about who I wanted to instruct. I did not know their family lawyer from a bar of soap. Perhaps it would have been better for them to have introduced me to him and leave me to think about it."*

IDEA #15

MAKE LUGGAGE TAGS OUT OF YOUR CLIENTS' BUSINESS CARDS

Some years ago I met an American speaker, Colleen Kaczor, at a conference. I gave her my business card when we met. Imagine my surprise a few weeks later when I received my card back in the mail, laminated as a luggage tag. On the back she had attached an inspirational quote. Some readers may think this tacky; as a recipient though, I thought it was a generous but simple gesture. I remembered her.

IDEA #16

CREATE YOUR OWN POSTCARD TO SEND TO CLIENTS AND CONTACTS

This is a fun way to personalise your communication with your clients and contacts. I have developed several postcards over the past couple of years, one of them using this cartoon I had previously commissioned from Wayne Logue, a talented cartoonist in New Zealand. I had used the cartoon as an overhead in some of my presentations. I simply took the artwork to a local printer and they converted it into a postcard. You will find that by ordering a minimum quantity of 500 they can work out as cheap to produce as business cards.

You could consider using a picture, a quote or a cartoon. Whatever you choose, a handwritten note on the card is important and is appreciated by most people.

IDEA #17

SEND BIRTHDAY CARDS

Do you like it when people you respect and trust send you a birthday card? I do! Why not return the compliment and send your clients and other important contacts a birthday card. Keep details about their birthdays on your database or in a birthday book.

IDEA #18
STOP SENDING CHRISTMAS CARDS
No doubt you receive hundreds of Christmas cards each year. Can you remember who sent them? Do you get embarrassed if you receive a card from someone you'd forgotten to include in your list, send one back by return mail only to find it arrives after the big day?

Why not avoid all the stress? Stop sending Christmas cards. Instead, send a card at a time of year when no-one else sends one. Consider sending a card to mark:

- New Year
- National Day
- Appointment of new partner (with their photo on the front of the card and an explanation of what they can do for clients)
- An award
- Your holiday

IDEA #19
GIVE CLIENTS YOUR HOME PHONE NUMBER
This is not necessarily a good idea if you are practising criminal law and value your time at home! However, it is a good idea if you want to show clients that you are available when they desperately need you. Clients will rarely call you at home but the fact that they can is a sign of great trust and helps build the relationship. In fact, when they do call you at home, you know you have successfully built one.

IDEA #20
REFER AND RECOMMEND OTHER RESOURCES
Be helpful to clients and recommend other service suppliers/products whenever you can. You do the client a favour by saving his/her time shopping around, you do the referrer a favour by introducing a new customer or client, so ultimately the favour will be returned. What you put out in life, you very often get back.

IDEA #21
GO THE EXTRA YARD

I knew of a legal executive who specialised in immigration law. As part of the service, he not only advised and processed immigration applications, he also booked accommodation for newly arrived immigrants and even drove to the local airport to greet his clients well into the evening. Now that was going the extra yard!

Here is a personal example. I was engaged to speak at a conference by a small company that manufactures essential oils for aromatherapy. The company had won government-backed awards for its business development. As a client, they were a delight to deal with before and during the conference. I was so impressed by their warmth, their attitude towards their distributors and by the simple courtesies extended to me that I invited them to feature on the front page of my newsletter, *Simon Says*. This offer was not part of our commercial agreement, just a simple gesture to acknowledge their professionalism; it helped me not just with a story for my newsletter but also helped to enhance the relationship with that client. They appreciated the offer. What can you do to go the extra yard with your clients?

IDEA #22
SUPPORT A CLIENT'S CHARITY

There are many reasons to give to charity—a desire to give something back to those less well off, a desire to feel you have contributed something and, of course, there's the tax deduction! Supporting charitable causes is always appreciated, especially if the charity is favoured by a client. While the Fred Hollows Foundation is not a client, $1 from the sale of every copy of this book will be donated to that charity. Why? Because it helps people and makes me feel I'm contributing in a small way to something worthwhile.

IDEA #23
HOST A "USER" CONFERENCE

Some firms are excellent at doing this. In an effort to be perceived as the legal experts in a given field (such as information technology, intellectual property, e-business, entertainment, etc), they host a conference to which their leading clients (or "users" as some organisations refer to them) in the industry are invited to attend and to speak. The effect is to create an event that is recognised in the industry as being a "must-not-miss". You can also use this event to invite prospective clients and representatives from the media. It accelerates the industry's perception of your firm and you being the expert in the field.

IDEA #24
OFFER CONVENIENT/FREE PARKING NEARBY YOUR OFFICE

I once interviewed a client of a law practice who said he was put off going to see his lawyers because they were downtown and parking was difficult. As a result of this comment, the law firm offered clients a complimentary pass to the public car park over the road from their office.

Before you start doing mental calculations about the cost of this exercise, consider first the value offered to your clients. Increase your value to them and you can increase your charges commensurately. You won't notice a negative difference to your bottom line, nor will your clients. It's the uncalled for extra; it's called "adding value".

ROD McGEOCH

Rod McGeoch is a former President of the NSW Law Society and led the bid for the Sydney 2000 Olympic Games. Today, he is Chairman of Corrs Chambers Westgarth in Sydney, Australia, and a highly regarded consultant and speaker.

Why did you choose a career in law?

I stumbled around not knowing what to do. I studied arts for a year but couldn't cope with it. After my modest effort in the first year, I then attended law school and loved it. I ended up being in the top 10 students. I loved the challenge of absorbing information. I discovered that one of my skills was my ability to simplify and explain matters to others.

Do you believe lawyers are doing enough to advance society?

Whenever is enough enough? I think it is wrong for people to suggest that lawyers are less than generous with their time. Like many other Australians who give their time to not-for-profit work, lawyers do a great deal—not to advance their careers but because they are motivated to help. There is an enormous amount of free legal aid work being done.

How important do you consider the contribution of the "behind the scenes" team in a law firm?

Behind the scenes staff are rewarded financially but they are not recognised. Unfortunately, many lawyers still view the "professional" and the "helper" differently. One of the strong criticisms I have of the profession, and to some extent of my firm, is that some partners see the HR director (for example) as just the person who hires a secretary! They do not see, nor recognise, the skills and expertise of such people who make a vital contribution behind the scenes.

What rewards do you find in your work?

They range from the financial to the satisfaction of trying to make a difference. There is also the issue of satisfying the ego. I think I would prefer to be successful and viewed as such in my profession, rather than not. I feel proud of the fact that, for over 30 years in the law, many people who have come to me for advice have gone away feeling grateful. That is very satisfying. My children's view, though, is that Dad's success has been a nuisance to them. They have found it to be intrusive occasionally.

How do you balance your work and your private life?

I've been very poor at developing balance in my life! These days I tell myself to stop work much earlier. I'm determined to change gears by the end of 2000. I'm doing it not just for my wife and children but also for myself. I want to improve that balance. A couple of years ago, my eldest daughter Lucy said, "You think that being a success in your career is success." I've never forgotten that. It was her way of saying that just because I was good at my job didn't mean I was good at being a dad! The problem for many lawyers is that they are too focused on seniority, success and promotion.

What are the secrets of your success?

My commitment to getting the job done. Whatever the task I have faced, I never felt that I wouldn't get there. Someone once said, "Your attitude determines your altitude," and I agree with that.

Lawyers have a tendency to think they are more important than they are. On the day I became leader of the Olympic bid, I recall the headline in the newspaper read "Rod Who?". There is an important message in this story to the legal community and that is that lawyers are a minor segment of the community at large and that the world will keep spinning on without them. For many people, the only time they will ever use a lawyer is when they buy a house or make a will. Lawyers therefore need to keep in perspective their value and place in the community.

Do you welcome the gradual erosion of the divisions between the professions?

I have no problem with it. I think that multi-disciplinary practices and one-stop shopping concepts are fine. They bring the hope of broader access to expertise with the prospect of a reduction in the costs. There are issues relating to conflict and privilege but these will get solved along the way. I don't see why lawyers should be restrained. I also think that in a market like Australia, professionals need to be careful about their profession remaining a viable unit. Australia is a small market and lawyers serve small markets. I believe that becoming part of bigger entities with international connections is the way to go.

These issues are of more immediate concern for the big firms. If I were in a small firm, I'd be wondering what the future held. Boutique practices excepted, small firms are facing a complete financial readjustment. I don't see them breaking the financial mould as the bigger firms have streaked ahead and the gap between the big firms and the small ones in terms of revenue generation is getting bigger. One problem I see for the larger firms is that there is no sense of relativity between what they earn and what ordinary people earn. The parties in the large firms these days demand high incomes without any sense of how much they really do earn.

Are lawyers greedy?

I think they have lost touch with what is reality "out there". They want to earn as much as other lawyers do, but they are no more materialistic than other successful people. I find that some lawyers are jealous of what other business people make. I think that even some of the people at our firm are 38 floors above reality! My time in the Olympic movement dealing with ordinary, excited people was a great lesson to me. We all need to understand our position in the world better and to appreciate that there are others out there such as teachers struggling on just $60,000 a year!

Is there one person who has inspired you beyond any others?

The greats such as the Kennedys, Churchills and Montgomerys of this world have all inspired me. I am an avid reader of writings and speeches and the people I find inspiring are those with a great sense of wisdom who can determine what is good and what isn't, and know what is to be done.

If you could do it all again, would you still choose to be a lawyer?

I can't think of doing anything else now that I know myself. The value it has given me in general attributes has been fantastic. I've had three great lives: one as a practising lawyer; then the Olympic Games bid; and subsequently I have had an enjoyable career on boards, consulting and speaking, a leadership role without doing any of the work. I promised myself after the Olympic bid that I would stay an international person and I have done that.

What advice would you give someone embarking on a legal career?

Recently, I was approached by a young lawyer who was asked me for some tips about how to advance his legal career. I gave him four tips: first, have a good attitude; second, do 'not for profit' work; third, go through every door and live a full life; and fourth, never let your skills wane. I think the business world is blind to the utility of our training. Lawyers offer competitive strategic thinking and I hope that the business world comes to recognise that fact.

CHAPTER 4

Connecting with New Clients

"If you wish in this world to advance
And your merits you're bound to enhance.
You must stir it and stump it,
And blow your own trumpet,
Or trust me, you haven't a chance."

GILBERT & SULLIVAN

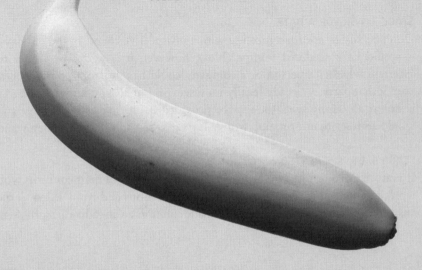

hile your main priority is developing new business from your existing clients, it's important that you devote time and effort to securing new business, especially when you are looking to improve the calibre of your client base (replacing your C and D clients and attracting more As and Bs).

In the previous chapter I discussed the importance of building relationships with clients. Building relationships in business is not too different from building them in your personal life. There is a courtship process involved, with (at least!) seven stages to the process:

STAGE 1: BE SELECTIVE ABOUT WHO YOU WANT

Be clear in your mind about the type of clients you would like to work for. If you open your doors to anyone, you'll be unlikely to attract quality clients. As David Maister writes,

> *"Act like a prostitute, with an attitude of 'I'll do it for the money, but don't expect me to care,' and you'll lose the premium that excellence earns."*

STAGE 2: LOOK ATTRACTIVE

Just as you might be self-conscious when going on a date, make that extra effort with prospective clients. That means paying attention to your clothes, grooming, manners and conversation. And make sure your office is tidy!

STAGE 3: ASK FOR A DATE

Don't be shy to ask for a meeting with a prospective client. In the old days, it would be considered touting. Now, however, it is perfectly proper to ascertain whether a person or a company could benefit from your services, even if that party is already legally represented. For all you know, that party is not at all happy with the service provided by their existing lawyer and would appreciate information from a lawyer who can offer what they want.

STAGE 4: BE INTERESTED

If you are not interested in the prospect and the nature of their concerns, you won't be interesting. Ask relevant, probing questions and really listen to the answers. Don't try to impose a ready-made solution on an individual problem.

STAGE 5: EMPATHISE

Don't go into a relationship thinking just what you can get out of it (e.g. 100 billable hours). Try and focus on what you can do to change the prospect's condition and how you can be most helpful to that person.

STAGE 6: REMEMBER THAT SIZE DOESN'T MATTER!

Many firms like to boast about the size of their practice ("We have 100 lawyers" or "We have affiliated offices in 100 countries"). While size, reflected by global connections, may be important for some corporate clients, what really matters to the client is that the lawyer relates to them as a human being, not just as another client who helps meet the lawyer's budget. It's not how big you are, it's how you use what you've got that matters!

STAGE 7. ASK, "HOW WAS IT FOR YOU?"

Having established a solid relationship with a client, you should be able and open enough to ask this question. In other words, did the quality of our work and service live up to your expectation? What can we do better? How would you like us to do that? Ideas 7-10 offer techniques to help you find the answers. Remember these stages, as they will help you through the courtship process. So will some of these ideas:

IDEA #25

TO GET HIRED, KNOW AND GO WHERE THE OPPORTUNITIES ARE

Robbers target banks because that's where the money is! Similarly, if you go fishing, you'll cast your line where the fish are. To find out where the opportunities are for you, simply put these questions to your A and B clients and prospects and listen to their answers:

- How did you hear about me?
- Who referred you?
- Why did you choose me to be your lawyer?
- Who has acted for you as your lawyer previously, if anyone?
- Do you have other lawyers currently acting for you?
- Is there any reason why you want different lawyers to act for you?
- Who is your accountant, financial planner, bank manager, real estate agent and doctor?
- Tell me about your business, its products and services
- What are the long-term and short-term goals of your business?
- What are the major challenges you face in your business?

- Who are your major competitors?
- How are you different from them?
- What have been the major achievements/setbacks in the past 12 months?
- What do you do well in your business?
- What would you like to improve in your business?
- What's most important to you when you need advice from a lawyer?
- What has to happen to make you feel that you are getting value for money?
- How can I help?

If these questions do reveal opportunities, don't be shy about asking for the business. As American business philosopher Zig Ziglar was once quoted as saying, "Timid salespeople have skinny kids!"

IDEA #26

DEVELOP A "SPOKEN LOGO"

Most buyers of your services couldn't care less about your firm's history, its size or smart premises. What they want to know is what your product or service will do for them. What is the emotional outcome for them? This needs to be reflected in all that you say about your services. This is particularly important when you are asked, "What do you do?" If you respond by saying, "I am a lawyer," you're just telling the inquirer what you are, not what you do. This is a wasted opportunity. Once you are clear about your value and the benefits you offer your clients, develop what Larry Schreiter, author of *The Happy Lawyer* (Shiloh Publications, 1999), calls your "spoken logo".

Apart from having the advantage of getting you to think about what you really contribute to the marketplace, a spoken logo can be a valuable tool to have up your sleeve when networking.

One of my clients, an accountant, when asked what she does, replies:
   "I take the hassle out of keeping books and records up to date for busy people who have better things to do."
A neat answer.

Here are some other simple examples for lawyers:

A family lawyer:
   "I divorce people," or "I help to finalise broken-down relationships amicably."

A conveyancing lawyer:
> *"I take the hassle out of buying and selling a home,"* or *"I make sure that when you buy a property, there are no hidden surprises."*

A commercial lawyer:
> *"I minimise the risk of my clients getting sued,"* or *"I help my clients negotiate profitable business transactions."*

These answers get straight to the point and enable the listener to know exactly what the benefit is to them of hiring you. They may well ask further questions to qualify you, such as "How do you do that?" At least it opens the door to a conversation rather than a polite but uninterested "Oh, really?"

This is not always an easy exercise to master. The more of a specialist you are, the clearer you will be about what you do for people, and the easier it will be to develop your spoken logo. If you are more of a generalist, you may find it helpful to develop several spoken logos, depending on your audience.

IDEA #27
ASK EXISTING CLIENTS FOR REFERRALS

The best way to find more of the same type of clients is through referral from existing clients who are delighted with the work you have done for them. Many of my clients tell me that they get up to 80% of their new business this way. However, lawyers do not devote the same percentage of their business development time or marketing budget to oiling the wheels of referral.

In my experience, most people in business don't ask for referrals. It's almost as though it is not polite to ask. However, just because you do not refer your suppliers to people you know doesn't mean you would not be prepared to do so if they asked, especially if you are pleased with the service they offer. After all, if you don't have confidence in them, why are using them in the first place?

My tip is to let those clients with whom you have a close relationship know how much you appreciate referrals and how important they are for the growth of your business. Don't assume they aren't happy to refer.

People will refer when they have confidence in you, because they trust you or because you have referred business to them. Assuming you are confident about your relationship with your client, you should have nothing to be embarrassed about.

IDEA #28
THANK ALL REFERRERS

Remember to reward or thank people for their introductions. It sounds obvious and while many lawyers appreciate referrals, they are often poor at expressing their appreciation. At its simplest, a phone call, a card or a letter saying two words will go a long way: THANK YOU!

You may wish to go further and send a bottle of wine, or a ticket to a play or movie. Approach your clients to see if they can supply any of these services. If purchasing from a non-client, explain to them what you are doing and ask who their lawyers are and whether they select goods for the same purpose from them. They might think twice next time about which lawyer to choose!

A note of caution is needed here. Some lawyers feel uncomfortable about giving or receiving any more than a thank you letter when they refer clients on to other professionals or accept referrals themselves. They consider giving or receiving gifts such as those mentioned above as potential bribes. Indeed, the issue of gifts and hospitality is a broad one and many people, notably those in the public sector, are governed by strict codes of conduct that determine whether gifts can or should be accepted. Law Societies also have their own rules about what is and is not acceptable.

In my view, if the gift is given as a sincere gesture rather than an overt attempt to unduly influence someone (or there is a risk that it might be perceived as such), then you are probably on safe ground. It is worth checking in advance on the company or public policy before inadvertently committing a faux pas!

IDEA #29
GET YOUR CLIENTS TO PASS ON A GIFT VOUCHER FROM YOU

Obviously, this idea is more appropriate for lawyers with a private client practice. Offer your clients a gift voucher for them to pass on to family or a friend which can be redeemed if they use your firm's services. You decide the value; for example, it could be worth $100 or a free half-hour consultation.

IDEA #30
BURN YOUR BROCHURES

Yes, that's right, chuck them in the bin or throw them on the fire! Sorry to annoy your design consultant, but most of the brochures produced by law firms that I have read might win some graphic designer an award and make the partners feel good, but beyond that they don't serve any other useful purpose.

When did your client last tell you they chose you because of your brochure? Brochures can work so long as they observe the rules outlined in the next three ideas.

IDEA #31
STROKE YOUR CLIENT'S EGO, NOT YOURS!

When I was working with an advertising agency in London, we had a client who insisted on advertising his business on his local television station. The main reason, it was rumoured, was not because his potential customers were likely to view the advertising; rather, it was so his wife could tell her friends that her husband's business appeared on television every evening! I'm not sure how much truth there was to this story, but it does illustrate the fact that, for many people in business, promotion has become an exercise in stroking the ego.

Let's take another look at the average law firm brochure. Typically, it will tell the reader how long the firm in question has been in business, how many people work for it, what services it offers and what smart premises it has. It may even feature pictures of partners vainly trying to look like pin-ups. Does this sound familiar?

Many brochures and other forms of similar egocentric promotion are nothing more than expensive exercises in corporate vanity. The focus is nearly always on the business, not on the prospect. The result is that the majority of promotional messages are boring, self-centred and fail to differentiate the business in the minds of the prospects. Importantly, they fail to appeal to the reader's concerns. If this sounds like your firm's promotional material, remove the egocentric aspects and start using messages that genuinely appeal to prospects.

E!

oose professional services on the basis of promotion alone.
ve said before, my research suggests that law firms get about 80% of their business as a result of word of mouth referral. However, the way you articulate your promotional message may make a difference when the prospect makes their choice. Focusing on the scope of your services, your commitment to excellent service or your ISO accreditation won't necessarily do you any favours, especially when your competitors can all offer exactly the same.

You need to give a prospect compelling reasons why you should be his favoured choice of lawyer. How can you do this?

IDEA #33
GIVE THE PROSPECT "REASONS WHY"

Understanding why your clients choose your business over the competition is the guts to the successful marketing of any business. That's why you always need to ask clients two questions: "How did you hear about us?" and "Why did you choose us?" (Another reason why your client feedback is so crucial.)

The first question is important because it will alert you to referrals and enable you to go back to the referrer with the appropriate acknowledgment of appreciation. Remember to create a field in your database called "referred by" for this specific purpose.

The second question is important because the answers will give you an indication about your point of difference. For example, if you are advertising your business in the Yellow Pages, don't waste your money on buying space to accommodate big logos or photographs of yourself. Nor should you place emphasis about your experience, expertise or state of the art technology when these are qualities that your prospects would expect from any lawyer. (Have a look at your local Yellow Pages and you'll see what I mean.)

Whatever medium you choose, make sure your message gives the reader/prospect reasons why they should choose you in preference to other firms. Your message needs to stand out from the herd, so the reasons need to be good ones. The next eight ideas offer some suggestions:

IDEA #34
BE UPFRONT WITH CLIENTS ABOUT YOUR FEES

The No.1 complaint I hear from clients is that lawyers don't always give clear estimates of their fees, or don't revise them when necessary. Some jurisdictions now make it mandatory for lawyers to do this. What a shame it has come to that. When you go to a restaurant you will be given a menu with prices attached. That's just what your clients want: transparency. Corporate clients, especially, have budgets to manage and by eliminating uncertainty about your fees, you make it easier for them to work with you.

IDEA #35
SELL VALUE, NOT TIME

I once knew a lawyer who believed he sold time. (I hope that wasn't his spoken logo!) He was convinced of it, and so are thousands of lawyers around the world. Lawyers do not sell time. Lawyers sell the benefits of what the client needs and buys. That may be peace of mind, financial security, corporate compliance, risk avoidance, happier lives, access to children, money from financial settlements, dispute resolution and so on.

The problem with billable time is that it places the emphasis on activity, not on value or results. Calculating your worth on an hourly basis is automatically self-limiting, because your time is only finite. For example if you bill 1,500 hours a year and your chargeout rate is $300 an hour, your maximum earning potential is restricted to $450,000 gross.

Yet it is possible to earn more than this if you focus on establishing fees based on value. How can you do this? Alan Weiss, author of *Million Dollar Consulting* (McGraw Hill, 1998,1992), offers five keys to establishing fees based on value:

1. Never quote a fee before you are ready to do so and have established what a successful outcome is worth
2. Establish conceptual value to the client rather than focusing on accounting for activities such as hours worked, reports prepared, photocopying, etc
3. Build the relationship with the right people—the decision-makers
4. If a client wants to negotiate you down, explain what value will be lost with each reduction of your fee
5. Be prepared to walk away from the business. As Weiss writes:

"One of the most fundamental distinctions of million dollar consultants compared to the rest of the field is their willingness to turn down business. The vast majority of consultants accept any assignment on the grounds that something is better than nothing. They ultimately relegate their professional lives to such-trade offs."

The nearest the legal profession has come to implementing this idea is to charge clients on a contingency basis. It may be high risk but it offers potentially high returns.

IDEA #36
GUARANTEE YOUR SERVICE STANDARDS—OR GIVE THEM THEIR MONEY BACK!

If you stand by the quality of your work (and most lawyers should do, they brag about it so often in their brochures) then be prepared to put your money where your mouth is and guarantee the quality of your service. (Note that I didn't say guarantee the outcome of a case.)

By offering a money-back guarantee, you remove the risk from the prospect's decision-making; the guarantee also makes a bold statement about your confidence in the quality of your service. Because not many other firms offer this, it is another reason to help you stand out from the herd. Gradually, as more firms do it, the weaker the impact will be. So do it now to give your business a competitive advantage. My business has been offering clients such a guarantee for several years and it has never once been called upon.

IDEA #37
OFFER CLIENTS EFTPOS AND CREDIT CARD FACILITIES FOR PAYMENT

The old-fashioned way of billing clients is to send an invoice to clients and await payment. Often, too much time is wasted on those C and D type clients who don't pay or can't pay. Why not collect payment as soon as you can and offer EFTPOS and credit card facilities? Not only is it a convenient way to pay, it also ensures you get paid promptly. There can be added benefits for clients in paying via their credit cards such as airline frequent flyer points.

IDEA #38
OFFER A HOLD-BACK PAYMENT SYSTEM

David Maister's excellent book *True Professionalism* reports that a number of corporations purchase their legal services on the proviso of a hold-back system. Using this approach, you bill your corporate clients the normal hourly rate but the client pays only 80% (or some such percentage) of your invoice, putting the remaining 20% into escrow. At the end of the year, your client reviews its satisfaction with all you have done and then decides how much of the remaining 20% to pay out. This is obviously useful when dealing with clients for whom you are doing on-going transactional work, not just one-off projects.

IDEA #39
OFFER PAYMENT BASED ON PERFORMANCE

Again, a tip from Maister. Suppose you are bidding for ongoing transactional work but the prospective client is fee-sensitive. Your reaction might be to discount your fees to get the work or stick to them and try and persuade the prospective client you are worth it. One way around this is to allow the prospective client to retain a percentage of your fee on condition that the balance is payable if you meet certain performance criteria. Additionally, you might also want to agree on a bonus payment should you exceed those criteria.

It takes courage to offer this to prospects because you relinquish control over a percentage of your fee to clients who can pay at their sole discretion. For some firms the commercial risk may seem too great. Yet this approach is far stronger than discounting an hourly fee rate.

IDEA #40
HIGHLIGHT THE TRUST FACTOR

You might feel proud of your firm's history and its track record; your firm has established a strong presence within the community and you believe this carries a lot of weight with clients. Is this a good reason to put to prospects?

I think it can be so long as you don't brag about it. Generally, the firm's history or longevity counts for little with prospects, many of whom are looking for relationships with individuals, not the firm. Trust is at the forefront of any business relationship, so turn your claim into a message that means something to a prospect. For example: "Generations of happy clients have placed their trust in us." If you personally have served many clients over the years, then consider making a similar claim: "Hundreds of happy clients have placed their trust in me."

CONTINUED ON PAGE 82

LARRY SCHREITER

Larry retired from legal practice to concentrate on offering clients financial tax and estate-planning advice. He is the author of The Happy Lawyer *and is based in the State of Washington, USA.*

Why did you choose to become a lawyer?
I saw lawyering as a way to become independently responsible for my own financial future while serving others.

Following the success of your excellent book 'The Happy Lawyer', what keeps you busy these days?
I realised that in 'The Happy Lawyer' I had summed up everything I had learnt about how to serve others in over 20 years. That in turn led to my actually retiring from law practice to embark on even greater service to clients through comprehensive financial, tax, estate and business planning with a major US financial planning firm.

Is there a motto that sums up your philosophy about life?
Serve first. I truly believe that through service to others and integrity in honouring them and their concerns, we do our profession proud.

Do you believe lawyers are doing enough to help advance society?
What will ever be enough? In the United States we have a strong tradition of adversarial justice, meaning the theory is that by each side contending vigorously for its position to prevail, ultimately society will benefit from the result. This is not always the case, however, as when forces of economic growth and prosperity and forces of environmental protection clash. I think the vector that results may tend in the long term towards advancement, but it is hard to always see that in the short run.
I do believe that the legal profession can take great pride in the advancements of the last 50 years in the areas of economic freedom, democracy and the like, but we have a long way to go to recognise true value and worth and distinguish it from petty self-aggrandisement, power-seeking and cut-throat litigation tactics, to the detriment of all conscientious lawyers.

How can lawyers change adverse public perception?
I believe that working to overcome the perception of an aloof elite by better

personal communications skills, such as I describe in my book, can help a great deal. On a larger scale, I feel attorneys should strive never to run down the profession, other lawyers, judges or anyone else in the system.

What can the leaders of the legal profession do to lay the foundations for the future?
Return to championing the foundations of individual liberty and freedom, and stop pandering to politically correct pressure groups.

What rewards do you find in your work?
Actually accomplishing results that benefit clients, their children and grandchildren, is a powerful reward.

What are the secrets of your success?
A stubborn streak of independence and never compromising my principles. Learning to say no. Also, turning down client work if it did not fit my values and goals, even if I earned less as a result.

Do you welcome the gradual erosion of the divisions between the professions?
It's too early to say, really, as in the US, the legal profession is regulated by each of the 50 States and in my State, for example, there is very little erosion as yet.

Are lawyers greedy?
Some are, some aren't. Certain high-profile attorneys certainly create that impression, yet no-one condemns professional athletes as greedy, despite their salaries of tens of millions of dollars for playing a game.

Is there one person who has inspired you beyond any others?
My Dad, to whom 'The Happy Lawyer' is dedicated. A small business owner, he showed me how to treat people, employees and customers both, while maintaining integrity and honesty and providing for his family and his future.

What advice would you give someone embarking on a legal career?
Dig down deep to discover their own values, and be sure the work they undertake does not lead them to undermine them. There is room in the legal profession for all who wish to serve.

CONTINUED FROM PAGE 79

IDEA #41
OFFER YOUR PROSPECTS AN INITIAL CONSULTATION

If you were considering buying a new car, you would want to take it for a test drive. Prospective clients who have not used your service before probably feel the same; they'd like to take you for a test drive to see if you match their expectations. Offer them a free initial consultation so you both have an opportunity to strike up a rapport. If an existing A client asks for a day of your time, be prepared to invest a day to build the relationship. Just charge for your expenses. This demonstrates a desire to collaborate to produce long-term results. It also enables the clients to feel they can call you without feeling they are being billed for every second you spend with them on the phone.

COLLABORATING WITH OTHERS

In connecting with new clients, you can save time and effort by sharing the load with other service providers. You can create an event or a promotion that serves everybody involved well. For example:

IDEA #42
RUN A JOINT SEMINAR/ADVERTISEMENT

I once read about a firm of real estate agents who teamed up with the local fire service and a firm that manufactured smoke alarms in New Zealand. It made for a clever, effective collaboration.

Consider how you could collaborate in joint promotional activities, such as seminars and newsletters, perhaps with a friendly accountant with whom you have a good relationship. You could jointly organise a seminar for your respective clients on a topic such as property investment and include a specialist in property investment and a financial planner. That way both the accountant and you get exposed to new prospects as well as offering something of value to existing clients.

IDEA #43
WRITE ARTICLES IN EACH OTHER'S NEWSLETTERS

This is an extension of the previous idea. There is a range of candidates with whom you could collaborate: for example, management consultants, non-competing lawyers, financial planners, funeral directors, real estate agents, environmental scientists, biotechnologists, stockbrokers, insurance agents, doctors, veterinary surgeons, clients and charities all offer opportunities.

IDEA #44
HIRE A PROFESSIONAL SPEAKER

Several years ago, when I was a marketing manager of a legal practice, I engaged the services of a top professional speaker who was an expert on marketing professional services. I hired him principally to help drive home a message to the lawyers I worked with that the responsibility for business development was as much theirs as mine. He charged a healthy daily fee but as I had previously heard him speak at a law society seminar, I was confident he'd hit the mark. However, I felt there was a slim chance my partners would be prepared to fork out the fee required to hear him speak for an hour or so. To make the exercise cost effective, I called an accountant friend and asked if he wanted to collaborate in the exercise. He jumped at the chance.

We both engaged the speaker for a day. In the morning, he gave two 90-minute speeches to the staff of each firm. In the afternoon, he gave a three-hour seminar to the invited clients and guests of both firms on how to earn more money in their businesses. Both my firm and the accountant's firm charged each guest a modest $50 to attend. The speaker's information was so valuable we could have charged guests double the admission price. Had we done so, we would have even made money out of this exercise (though that was not the objective).

Overall, we virtually covered the costs of the exercise, our respective firms had the benefit of a private session with a high-profile speaker, and our invited guests were delighted. On top of that the speaker got paid his full fee!

You can find a listing of professional speakers who are experts in their respective fields on the following websites:
United States of America: www.nsaspeaker.org
Australia and New Zealand: www.nationalspeakers.asn.au
United Kingdom: www.professionalspeakers.org

IDEA #45
BECOME A PROFESSIONAL SPEAKER!

The world is crying out for people who can speak confidently about their area of expertise. Next time you are asked to speak at a client's conference, you could consider charging them a fee rather than doing it for free. My legal experience as a criminal advocate has been invaluable in building my business as a professional speaker. If you want to learn more about this exciting industry, I suggest you read two contrasting yet inspiring books, *Speak and Grow Rich* by Dottie and Lilly Walters (Prentice Hall, 1997) and *Money Talks* by Alan Weiss (McGraw-Hill, 1998).

IDEA #46
ASK FOR—AND USE—TESTIMONIALS

Testimonials are rarely used in law firm marketing. Other than to protect the identity of clients, I can think of no other good reason not to use them (other than clients being reluctant to give them!). Of course, like referrals, unsolicited testimonials are always the best. Yet these days, while clients may genuinely appreciate the service that has been given and are prepared to recommend you, few have the time to sit down and put pen to paper. So, ask clients who give you good feedback if they would be prepared to put it in writing. Offer to write the testimonial yourself if necessary, send it to them for their approval and ask them to put it on their letterhead. You can use testimonials in a dossier in reception for clients to read, as endorsements for promotional literature (newsletter, brochure and advertising) and as part of a credentials document such as a proposal. They are very worthwhile because they give confidence to the prospect.

A testimonial should not just say what a nice person, firm or practice you are. It should state how easy you were to work with, how you finished the project on time and within the budget, and what the client gained as a result of your work.

IDEA #47
WRITE ARTICLES

To be perceived as an expert in your field, you must establish your credibility. Easy-to-read, published articles are an excellent way to do this. Submit them to industry associations whose members are your target market. Also submit them to editors of magazines or journals that might be read by your target market. Do not be pressured into buying advertising space in their magazine as a condition of publication. Good public relations are not about paying for exposure but getting it for free. Conversely, get them to pay you for your articles! When you get published for a fee, then you become positioned as the expert.

IDEA #48
WRITE A BOOK

If you want to skyrocket your credibility, write and publish a book, or co-author a book as part of a collaboration. You can either publish or self-publish; I know people who have gone down both paths and have experienced pros and cons with each. There are a couple of very useful resources written by people who know the industry inside out: *The Self Publishing Guide* by Dan Poynter (ISBN 1-56860-059-3), and *Publish for Profit* by Cyndi Kaplan (ISBN 0-646-30239-6).

IDEA #49
GET (FAVOURABLE) MEDIA EXPOSURE

Every day, news and feature editors of newspapers and radio shows are searching for stories, particularly local news and human interest issues.

Consider making an authoritative statement in the media commenting on some legal developments, or translating a complicated judgment into a simple form. These are good ways to make it into the media. Some lawyers get a regular spot on the radio, be it a pre-recorded three-minute weekly comment or as a guest on talkback radio; alternatively, they write a regular column in the appropriate press. Sometimes they are at the top of an editor's list to call for comment on particular developments. Think about what options best suit you and consider using a public relations agency to steer you in the right direction. Remember, newspapers are not interested in publishing stories that are unpaid advertorials for your business. Here are 12 genuine newsworthy angles:

- Appointments
- Professional industry comment
- Research
- Controversial cases
- Relocation
- Facts and figures
- Awards and achievements
- Special events
- Success stories
- Community/charity events
- "How to" information
- Sponsorships

IDEA #50
WRITE A PRESS RELEASE

This work is better suited to a professional public relations person than a lawyer. If you have to do it yourself, here are some tips:

- Research the publication's writing style and write your article in the same manner
- Make a list of the appropriate media and the names of contacts such as editors and reporters
- Make sure the topic is relevant and current to the industry
- Add "Media Release" to the top of your letterhead for press releases
- Fax press releases, don't post them
- Be aware of deadlines
- Be available for comment by phone
- Create a headline with appeal
- Keep it short and to the point
- Include your contact details at the bottom.

Remember to send your clients copies of all (favourable) published articles.

IDEA #51
PRODUCE PUNCHY PROFILES AND PERSUASIVE PROMOTIONAL MATERIAL

Firms are increasingly being asked to take part in "beauty parades" and submit tenders. Some firms are now deciding not to go down this path to source new work as it is time-consuming and is not a basis for a collaborative relationship. The challenge is to build relationships that demonstrate you care about a prospect's business rather than having to go through the motions and pretend that you do in a tender document!

However, in non-competitive scenarios, it is always useful to have some punchy profiles or persuasive promotional material on hand.

If a prospect does ask you to submit a written proposal, do not do so until you have established with the prospect what his or her objectives are. Then structure your proposal to include the following details:

Introduction
This is what your reader is going to read. Make sure you thank the reader for the opportunity to submit the proposal.

Your understanding
Demonstrate you understand your reader's legal needs.

Your value
State clearly what you can do for them.

The people involved
Explain who will do the work; profile their experience, expertise and involvement in the prospective client's industry.

What's different about your firm
The truth is, there is very little to distinguish one major firm from another. A lawyer friend told me recently that while his firm took part in a beauty parade, he was frank enough to tell the prospect that there was little difference between the service his firm could offer and that of the others who were also being considered. He went on to tell the prospect that what did differentiate his firm was its loyalty to its clients and that if selected, there would be no risk in being "dumped" because of a conflict of interest. His firm was not chosen initially. However, the firm that was selected subsequently declared a conflict of interest and was unable to represent the client. Guess who got a call from the client? My lawyer friend of course!

Explain the level of service they can expect
Detail the level of communication and service standards as well as any guarantees offered.

Costing and timing
Indicate how long it will take to implement activities, what the anticipated costs will be, and what you propose to charge. Suggest options for billing. (Go for the prospect's preference, not yours!)

Referees/testimonials
Include them. They will endorse and support your case.

Ask for the business
Tell them, "We want your business."

Remember to write in their language. Avoid using pompous words, jargon and Latin.

IDEA #52
GIVE POWERFUL PRESENTATIONS

How often have you sat through a speech and been bored out of your mind? What kind of impression did the presenter make? Not great, I'm sure! Unfortunately, there are many lawyers who are experts in their field but who are hopeless at presenting in front of an audience. This is an increasingly important social and business skill. Unless you learn it, you risk letting yourself down and losing out on business opportunities. This need not happen to you if you follow some very simple steps:

First, you must understand that the secret to a sensational presentation is to deliver the steak with sizzle and style; in other words, be knowledgeable, sound interesting and look good. Let me briefly deal with each in turn.

Be knowledgeable

Imagine you are scheduled to present in front of an audience because you have something important to tell them. (If you haven't, you shouldn't be giving the presentation in the first place!) In shaping your presentation, ask yourself this question: "What is the single most important message I want this audience to take away with them?" Be clear about your overall objective. Try to boil down your technical information to three or five key points. That way, the information is more accessible for the audience. Many professionals are often asked to deliver a paper. Your challenge is not to deliver a paper; if all you do is read out a paper that the audience can read anyway, you might as well not be there. It is a terrible turn-off. If the information you are sharing with your audience is of a highly technical nature, distribute your information in a paper or article to the audience at the end of your presentation.

Sound interesting

Knowing what you want to say is one thing; knowing how to say it is another. I am often asked how to spice up a presentation that is full of dry and potentially mind-numbing information. People respond to what they can see, sense, touch, smell and hear. The challenge for you is to appeal to some or all of those senses during your presentation. Here are some ideas to help you:

Use stories and anecdotes

Ever since we were children we have enjoyed being told stories. Stories that can illustrate your point, perhaps relating to case studies of clients or even referring to a personal experience, will always reinforce your presentation.

Refer to interesting sources of information

Referring to a story in the day's newspaper, to a passage in a book or to a research report will help paint a picture in the minds of the audience. I regularly use famous or inspiring quotes in my presentations to illustrate a point.

Use humour

Some presenters think that being on a platform gives them carte blanche to be a stand-up comedian. Invariably, this approach seriously backfires. If you are naturally funny, it will come across as part of your personality. I suggest you use amusing quotations to help you. There are many collections of these available in your local bookstore.

Sound interested and look good

I have often witnessed speakers who look bored, present in a monotonous voice and say "er" and "um" throughout their presentation. Again, it's a terrible turn-off. Focus on the following:

Look smart

Naturally it is important to be well-groomed and smartly dressed if you are on the platform.

Make eye contact

Don't stare at members of your audience, as this will make them feel un-comfortable. Vary your eye contact to different members of the audience, ideally those whom you have met in advance of your presentation.

Present with or without notes

It doesn't matter whether you make your presentation with or without notes. If you know your stuff well enough and can present without reference to notes and without hanging on for dear life to a lectern, it will reinforce in the audience's mind the perception of someone who is an expert: at ease and confident.

Be audible

First, you must be heard. If your voice is weak, make sure you are using a microphone. Second, vary the pitch so your voice is not monotonous. Third, vary the rhythm so the pace is slow in some parts and faster in others. Think of television sports commentators!

Pause
Do not feel you need to speak all the time. Pausing and creating a few seconds of silence after making an important point gives the audience time to digest what you have said and gives you time to mentally and physically draw breath!

Involve the audience
Asking questions such as "Can I see a show of hands?" gets the audience working with you. Just asking them to share an idea with the person sitting next to them can break the ice and remove the focus from you for a short while. Perhaps you might want a volunteer from the audience to help you with a demonstration. This can create a lot of amusement in a presentation.

Understand how the technical equipment works
I have lost count of the number of times I have seen presenters lose their credibility because they don't know how to use microphones, Power Point or overhead projectors. If you are relying on audio/visual equipment as part of your presentation, it pays to be totally familiar with it.

Success as a presenter won't happen overnight but if you put these tips into practice you will be well on your way.

IDEA #53
GO TO ONE NETWORKING FUNCTION A WEEK
You won't meet prospects sitting on your backside in the office! Schedule time to attend client industry association meetings and business groups such as your local Chamber of Commerce. At those functions you have the opportunity to meet new prospects and develop new relationships. Take your business cards with you. Do what Robyn Henderson, Australia's networking specialist and author of *How to Master Networking* (Prentice Hall, 1997), suggests:

> *"Go to a networking function at least once a week. Make it easy for people to do business with you. Always follow up with the people you meet."*

IDEA #54
USE BOTH SIDES OF YOUR BUSINESS CARDS
Most lawyers' business cards look the same. They show the firm's name in the biggest letters, the lawyer's name halfway down with his status (partner,

senior associate) below his name. It then lists the phone and fax numbers in a smaller font size, with the email and any website address in even smaller letters. The flip side is blank. If your card is like this, consider making the following modifications.

- Put the your direct dial number underneath your name or in bold. That's the reason why people keep your card—so they can call you. How many times have you dialled a fax number by mistake, because the phone and fax were indistinguishable from each other?
- Your card should tell people what you do, not just what you are. Rather than stating partner, lawyer or senior associate, spell out your area of expertise, e.g. tax specialist. Even better, include your spoken logo.
- Use the flip side of your card to give useful information. For example, "How to find us" with a street map printed on the back; your spoken logo; or a list of your firm's other specialty areas.
- Print your photograph on the front. Not because you are necessarily model material but because your photo helps people to remember you. This works for thousands of business people.
- List the names of the professional bodies or networks you belong to. This will help you connect with other members of the same organisation.
- Have more than one card for different occasions or different clients.

IDEA #55
BE CONSIDERATE TO YOUR SUPPLIERS

Your business success depends, to a certain extent, on the quality of your suppliers. These are the people in organisations who supply you with your stationery, computer hardware and software, furniture, cars, confectionery, toilet paper, alcoholic beverages, graphic design, newsletters, elevators, office space, photocopiers, printers, telephone service and your people (recruitment consultancy). Who does the legal work for them? Perhaps they have other customers to whom they might refer you? Your suppliers are a potent source of new business if you go looking for it. Be considerate to your suppliers and they will be considerate to you.

IDEA #56
TAKE YOUR PLACE IN CYBERSPACE!

The world of information technology is changing even as I write this paragraph! Save to say, email and websites have become important communication and promotional tools. There are many experts who can advise on setting up the appropriate systems to meet your needs. Don't use your website as another glorified brochure—use it to market and position you differently from other firms. Don't copy theirs, rather, learn from them. It is worth paying an expert to help you make the most of the opportunities here.

IDEA #57
BECOME A SPONSOR

You may want to sponsor a charity, a cause or a function that will give you favourable exposure. Make sure you appreciate the difference between a charitable donation and a sponsorship agreement. The former is simply a donation; the latter may entitle you to names, addresses and naming rights.

IDEA #58
OFFER TO SPEAK AT YOUR CLIENT'S INDUSTRY ASSOCIATION CONFERENCES

Many lawyers' idea of networking is to rub shoulders with peers. That doesn't win any business. Your presence as a speaker at an industry or association meeting of a client or potential client demonstrates your interest, positions you as an expert in that field, and gets you networking with a wide range of potential clients. You'll find there won't be many other lawyers in the room! Once you have established yourself with that group as a speaker, start charging a fee to speak. Who knows where that could take you? Generally, effective business speakers are in the $5,000 to $10,000 range for an engagement.

IDEA #59
TURN YOUR OFFICE INTO A COFFEE SHOP

Close to my office is a shop that sells books and serves coffee. Some people might call it a cafe with a bookstore attached. It is in fact a bookstore with a small espresso bar serving coffee to customers while they peruse the latest books on the shelf. Why not be different and turn your office into something similar? Too ridiculous for words you think? Well, at the Lakewood Shopping Centre in East Dallas, Texas, lawyer David Musslewhite has done just that and turned his office into a coffee shop. Legal Grounds Law and Coffee is now succeeding as both a cafe and a law firm!

PAT O'SHANE

Pat was the first Aboriginal female teacher in Queensland, the first Aboriginal person in Australia to graduate in law and the first woman to head a government department—the Department of Aboriginal Affairs in 1984. Pat practised as a barrister and today she is a leading magistrate in NSW, Australia.

Why did you choose to become a lawyer?

When I was 21, I was teaching in the far north of Queensland and I was very active in the Aboriginal Advancement League. In 1962, there was an incident when a couple of thoroughly intoxicated police officers went to an Aboriginal reserve. They burst down the door of the cottage and assaulted two 15-year-old Aboriginal women. Someone from the reserve came to my home in Cairns to complain about the officers' behaviour. I took her into the city and got her to press charges in the Court of Petty Sessions. What angered me was the way in which the assaulted women were regarded as the perpetrators and the men the victims. I thought then that one day I would do something to help women like that.

At that stage, I didn't know I would be a lawyer, nor did I have any concept of law other than the way in which the police treated Aborigines and unionists. I continued teaching until I was in my 30s. I was sent to Sydney for some medical treatment and I had it in my mind then to study medicine. A friend there suggested I consider studying law, which revived my interest in it. My motivation was the strong sense of injustice I had experienced all my life. This was reinforced by what I saw was happening in Australia; for example, the arrests over Vietnam, censorship, and Aboriginal rights.

Do you believe there is an adverse public perception of lawyers?

I think it is true that there is a negative public perception of lawyers, generated by the view that so many lawyers are greedy. But there are many, many lawyers who go into law out of altruistic motivation. They want to help people. Many of them have a strong sense of justice; they want to bat for the underprivileged and dispossessed, but their efforts often pass unheralded.

How can lawyers change adverse public perception?

A couple of years ago, the Law Society in Sydney ran advertisements on commercial television. Some also appeared in community newspapers. Those ads were about the fact that people could get free, or at least less expensive, representation through a pro-bono scheme. I think that lawyers would do some good by advertising that scheme more. Also, I believe that Bar Associations and Law Societies could make practitioners available in schools where law studies are taught. It's a two-way street. Schools and teachers are unaware that lawyers would be prepared to go to schools.

Are lawyers greedy?
Greed is the ethos of the day. Other professionals in other tightly constrained professions are greedy. What a lot of people don't realise is how much work is involved in being a lawyer. Much of it is hidden. Lawyers are entitled to be recompensed for that work. Lots of people, I believe, think court advocacy is a doddle. We are dealing with very important legal matters, and often quite complex issues of evidence law. There are principles that have to be established. Lots of people don't understand why certain laws of evidence exist. Many people take rumour to be gospel; where someone's liberty is at stake, then that's a serious step to take. Therefore strict rules of evidence are necessary. There is a lot of work in lawyering and so lawyers should be paid their due.

What can lawyers do to advance society?
While I have done no research into it, I think there has been a major change in the last 25-30 years. It started in the 1970s when community legal centres were set up and had practising lawyers and students observing police behaviour, especially towards Aborigines in Redfern, Sydney. Many lawyers in Australia are concerned with trying to change our society to a civil, democratic one that has appropriate regard for human as well as social and political rights. So, yes, I do think that they are doing a lot to advance society. Some spend all their time doing just that!

What rewards do you find in your work?
I try to do the best I can for people around me. I try to set high standards of behaviour. There's a fine line between use and abuse of power and it is up to people like lawyers (and myself) to ensure that there are brakes on the substantial powers of the institution of the police. That is the satisfaction I get; I'm making a positive contribution to society. That's all I need to feel.

Is there a motto that sums up your philosophy about life?
Do unto others as you would have done unto you.

CHAPTER 5

Connecting with Your People

"Convention dictates that a company looks after its shareholders first, its customers next and last of all worries about its employees. Virgin does the opposite ..."

SIR RICHARD BRANSON, FOUNDER AND CHAIRMAN, THE VIRGIN GROUP

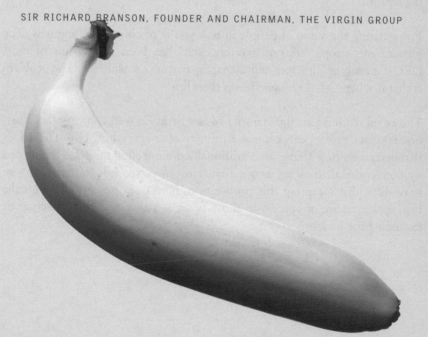

C onvention dictates that a company looks after its shareholders first, its customers next and last of all worries about its employees. Virgin does the opposite. For us, our employees matter most. It just seems common sense to me that, if you start off with a happy, well-motivated workforce, you're much more likely to have happy customers. And in due course, the resulting profits will make your shareholders happy."

SIR RICHARD BRANSON, FOUNDER AND CHAIRMAN, THE VIRGIN GROUP

In June 1984, I was fortunate to be aboard *Maiden Voyager* on its inaugural flight for Virgin Atlantic from London to New York. It was an exciting and memorable day and I felt as though I was witnessing history in the making. Probably, I was, as since then, Virgin Atlantic has grown to be the jewel in the crown for the Virgin Group, an organisation that has now become one of the most visible and successful companies in Britain. It has also earned itself a reputation as being one of the best to work for. Perhaps this is a reflection of its founder's philosophy, which places emphasis more on satisfying the people associated with its business rather than just on generating a profit.

Emphasising the value of people in business is of course nothing new. The phrase "our people are our greatest asset" has been on the lips of most CEOs, managing directors and managing partners worldwide. The problem is that is where it has remained—on their lips!

The awful truth is that the majority of law firms (as well as most other businesses) place profit generation as a priority over everything else. The values that determine how things are traditionally done around the place are shaped by conventional thinking: profit first, customers second, staff last. If you have difficulty accepting this proposition, how does one explain why the principal measure of success in those firms is a financial one—meeting or exceeding the budget?

It is hardly surprising that if meeting budget is the prime measure of success, people will focus all their energies on activities that support that objective. Just when they need to focus their energies in other areas, it is clear that it is time law firms should start to think differently about their priorities.

THE COST OF TURNOVER

For example, the cost of not treating people as your most important asset is considerable. A recent study carried out on behalf of the Victoria Law Foundation in Australia found that the turnover cost to a firm when an experienced lawyer leaves and is replaced is approximately $150,000. On that basis, there must be many firms who are losing well over several million dollars a year in this way. The cost has to be paid for by somebody—presumably the clients or the partners.

Measuring the costs of people leaving a firm may be a powerful reminder of the value of those people but understanding the causes behind a person's decision to leave is critical. Many firms have a system of exit interviews to help them understand what those causes might be. Money isn't always the answer.

> *"The two most common reasons for leaving a job which we hear is that the lawyer they work with shows them no appreciation or that they are treated abruptly or rudely."* Deborah Zurnamer

The American Bar Association Young Lawyers Division in 1990 conducted possibly the most comprehensive study of lawyer dissatisfaction. More than 3,000 lawyers under the age of 36 or having less than three years experience were interviewed, and they cited three major causes of job dissatisfaction:

• Lack of time for self, family and friends owing to billable hours requirements
• Poor communication and isolation within the firm
• Lack of training and mentoring within the firm.

CONNECTING WITH YOUR PEOPLE

Consider the two columns below: each lists the attributes of two types of firm. The one on the left is the type of firm that connects with its people whereas the one on the right fails to.

CONNECTING PARTNERS	MISFIRING PARTNERS
• Strive for excellence	• Tolerate mediocrity
• Trust people with autonomy	• Rule and regulate
• Co-operate with each other	• Are bureaucratic
• Look for solutions	• Look for problems
• Earn loyalty	• Try to buy loyalty by offering high salaries
• Are genuinely interested in their people	• Pay lip service to training and development

CONNECTING FIRM	MISFIRING FIRM
• Creative	• Mechanistic
• Dynamic	• Passionless
• Full of risk takers	• Devoid of ideas
• Courageous	• Cowardly
• Challenging	• Conformist

FIRED-UP PEOPLE	DIRECTIONLESS PEOPLE
• Pursue their passion	• Pursue their pension
• Are loyal	• Are disloyal
• Are trusted	• Are not trusted

Is yours a connecting firm or a misfiring one?

I hope I have made the point by now that to connect with people, firms must let people be themselves. I am not advocating an idealistic "we're one big happy family" culture. There is too much diversity in a legal practice for that to ever occur. However, firms that rely on accreditation programs or policy manuals to promote harmony, loyalty and cohesion are doomed to fail. Such techniques simply will not capture the hearts and minds of the people. As Brazilian industrialist Ricardo Semler, author of the best-selling business book *Maverick* (Century, 1993), writes, "They strip away freedom and give nothing in return but a false feeling of discipline and conformity."

So how can firms connect more with their people?

IDEA #60
WORK TOGETHER LIKE ANY SPORTING TEAM

Everybody who works in the business, from the person in the mail room to the senior partner, is part of your team. For teams to work cohesively, all team members need to work together. As in any sporting team, you may have your stars, but every star needs the support of his or her team members to achieve their success. (Let's not forget that good teams also have raving fans who pay their money regularly and support the club!)

IDEA #61
ELIMINATE FEAR FROM THE WORKPLACE

After post-graduate studies, when I worked in the advertising agency, a new chief executive was appointed. The first thing he did was to fire some 50 people who were considered excessive to the organisation's requirements. Needless to say, the effect of his actions had a demoralising effect on staff. By creating an atmosphere of fear, it motivated staff to do one thing—justify their existence and hang on to their jobs. That chief executive didn't last long.

IDEA #62
START LEADING OR CONSIDER LEAVING

Historically, partnership has not been synonymous with leadership, but it should be. Many partners have attained their partnership status not so much on merit but by default or by being one of the boys (which perhaps explains why so few of the girls have become partners!). In the progressive legal business of today, there is no longer room at the top for partners who are passengers.

Many books have been written on leadership, but one that stands out is Napoleon Hill's *Think and Grow Rich* (Fawcett, 1960). Hill's work is a monument to individual achievement and is regarded as the cornerstone of modern motivation. For three decades Hill studied, interviewed and inter-preted the habits, attitudes and know-how of great achievers—brilliant inventors such as Thomas Edison and powerful businessmen such as Andrew Carnegie.

According to Hill, a true leader is someone who:

1. Is courageous
2. Has self-control
3. Has a keen sense of justice
4. Is decisive
5. Plans his work and works his plan
6. Does more than he's paid for
7. Has a pleasing personality
8. Is sympathetic and understanding
9. Masters detail
10. Is co-operative.

These are excellent qualities to nurture and to demonstrate to your people.

"Leadership is all about encouraging people to have trust and confidence in you."

DAVID LANGE, FORMER PRIME MINISTER OF NEW ZEALAND

IDEA #63
GET TO KNOW ALL YOUR PEOPLE
In one firm I encountered, one employee told me how she had gone into the mail room where a partner introduced himself to her, asked who she was, and said he hadn't seen her around the office before. She told him her name and announced she had in fact been with the firm for two years!

On another occasion, during a survey, I asked a group of junior lawyers to name one thing that their employers might do to improve their performance. One lawyer wrote back, "It would be nice if my supervisor would remember my name"!

The moral of the stories: make sure you know who is working on your team.

IDEA #64
ABOLISH PARTNER-ONLY LUNCHES
Partner-only lunches are elitist and reinforce the "them and us" culture that is associated with hierarchical partnerships. Instead, open up the doors of

the boardroom to everyone—senior associates, articled clerks, para-legals, secretaries, receptionist, telephonists, mail deliverers and the whole management team. Make sure the partners don't all huddle together. Get them talking with the most junior and the newest recruits to the team. Check that they are taking a sincere interest in them.

IDEA #65
MAKE YOUR TEAMS RESPONSIBLE FOR MANAGING THEIR BUDGETS
Many firms are broken down into divisions around areas of expertise. These divisions should be treated as business units and given the financial resources to grow their business. By all means make them responsible and accountable, but allow them to decide how best to manage their budget. It should not be necessary for them to get clearance every time they want to spend money on business development activities.

IDEA #66
TRUST YOUR PEOPLE
I recall speaking with an associate of a private practice who complained to me about the lack of trust the managing partner had in him and other more junior colleagues. Apparently, his managing partner would walk around the office after lunch at 2.10pm checking that he and others were not taking extended lunch breaks and were getting on with the business of billing! Assuming that people are being hired because of their capabilities, they should then be trusted to get on with the job.

IDEA #67
RECRUIT PEOPLE FOR PERSONALITY FIRST
Many advertisements for job vacancies emphasise the need for candidates to possess certain years of experience or to have particular expertise. There are plenty of people around who might qualify. However, clients want lawyers who can communicate with them and who are likeable people, not just smart boffins! Therefore when recruiting staff, prioritise your selection criteria by looking firstly for personality, secondly for skills and knowledge, and lastly for experience.

IDEA #68
DRESS UNCONVENTIONALLY
It is becoming more acceptable to go to work in smart but informal clothes. The suit is out for many professionals. Some firms now make it a policy to

allow staff to wear casual clothes on Fridays. Why just Fridays I wonder? If it's good enough for Friday, why is it not good enough for every day of the week? Having worked in the legal profession and the advertising industry, it interested me to see how differently their respective senior people dress. Organisations from both industries sometimes share the same clients, charge a high rate for their services and yet dress very differently. Richard Branson is widely regarded as Britain's most admired businessman. When did you ever see him in a suit and tie?

IDEA #69
RESPECT YOUR MANAGEMENT TEAM

Firms are spending a great deal of money hiring highly skilled people to support them in management roles; consider this list (which continues to grow as roles evolve):

- Chief executive officer
- Practice manager
- Business development manager
- Marketing manager
- Client relationship manager
- Events co-ordinator
- Human resources manager
- Training and development manager
- Information and technology manager
- Knowledge and information manager

These people do a tremendous job and yet openly confess to feeling frustrated by the occasional disrespectful attitude exhibited towards them by the lawyers they serve. Many state they do not have a voice within their organisations. In a survey of Australian law firms carried out by my business, law firm marketers were asked what they would ask for, given one wish by a magic genie. The answer: a culture change in lawyers' attitudes towards client service, marketing and business development. Whenever that happens, law firm marketers might even find themselves out of a job!

Learn to recognise your limitations and to surrender control over management decisions to those who are qualified and who are paid so to do. And bear in mind the old saying, "A solicitor who acts for himself has a fool for a client."

IDEA #70
BECOME A SUCCESSFUL DELEGATOR

What percentage of your work could be handled by someone less experienced than yourself? Typically in my seminars, the percentage among delegates is sometimes upwards of 50%. This is not an efficient state of affairs, nor is it good for you, because you will find yourself doing tasks that someone with your experience should not be doing, and the desire to do it all yourself deprives a less experienced person of the opportunity to learn. Consider the tasks that you normally undertake at home and at work and identify those that can be delegated. By becoming a more effective delegator, you will free up more time and make life a little easier. Avoid the temptation to do it all yourself and practice the next two ideas.

IDEA #71
GIVE CLEAR INSTRUCTIONS

Specifically, make sure the person to whom you are delegating understands:

- The background to each assignment
- What you want them to do
- How much time they should spend on each assignment
- When they should report back
- Where to get help, e.g. what information resources are available
- Who is responsible for what, e.g. dealings with client.

Taking the time to do this will save you a lot of time correcting mistakes later on. Give the younger members of your team the checklist in Appendix D. After giving instructions, ask them to describe to you what they are supposed to do, using the phrase, "to make sure I explained it clearly".

IDEA #72
GIVE AND ASK FOR FEEDBACK

This is the second crucial part of being a successful delegator. My research confirms that this is an area where supervisors seriously under-perform and yet it is one aspect of their learning that young lawyers value most. Don't think feedback is something that can wait until an annual appraisal. It is an ongoing process. Make sure it is

- Constructive—focus on the positives first

CONTINUED ON PAGE 106

DEBORAH ZURNAMER

In the past 13 years, Deborah not only moved from South Africa to Australia, she also stopped practising law and established Law Personnel, a very successful legal recruitment company in Sydney, Australia.

Why did you stop practising law?
When I made the decision to leave the law, I was juggling work, lectures (and exams) to convert my qualification as well as being a recently separated single parent, all of which was emotionally and physically debilitating. At the time, I only intended to have a temporary absence but I suppose subconsciously I saw it as an opportunity to explore other options. I don't think I ever thought I would practice law forever. I always had this love-hate relationship with the law—when I was in it I wanted to be out of it and when I was out I really missed being a part of it.

What rewards do you find in your new line of business?
It's great to work within the profession without having to practise. I feel like all the years of study, experience and knowledge of the industry have not been a waste. I can use it all to assist others in securing work within the legal environment. I've been there, done that, so I can advise candidates about the advantages and pitfalls. It is very rewarding when I see them reaping the rewards of taking a job that really fulfils them. In addition, I have the variety of being involved in recruitment, marketing, business development and counselling—and the opportunity to enjoy the friendships of incredibly interesting and motivating people.

How important do you consider the contribution of the "behind the scenes" team in a law firm?
The "behind the scenes" team is essential to the day-to-day success of any law firm. The problem is that lawyers don't really want to know how it is being done, they just want a result. I hear and see the frustrations of this team daily. Personally, I don't see them getting sufficient recognition and rewards to justify the frustrations of the job.

How can lawyers change adverse public perception?
Perhaps the most important thing is overcoming the arrogant "them and us" mentality. Approachability and showing the "human side" is sometimes lacking.

Interestingly, the two most common reasons for leaving a job that we hear from people we place is that the lawyer they work with shows them no appreciation, or that they are treated abruptly or rudely. What many lawyers don't realise is that the employees who leave for these reasons tell other firms and the public about this, and the reputation for arrogance is perpetuated.

What are the secrets of your success?
Integrity, professionalism, tenacity, sense of humour and empathy. Most importantly, I try to treat people the way in which I would like to be treated.

How do you balance your work and your private life?
One of the aims of starting my own business was to achieve a balance in my life and this extends to other people who work with me. I realised a long time ago that working smarter instead of longer always achieved the best results for me—and it continues to do so. The other thing I am slowly learning is to say no to commitments that I know will destroy this balance.

Do you welcome the gradual erosion of the divisions between the professions?
It think it was inevitable. For the clients, it provides an integrated solution to a multi-faceted matter.

Are lawyers greedy?
I think the legal profession is no different from any other—some lawyers are greedy and some aren't.

Is there one person who has inspired you beyond any others?
My mother, who passed away when I was 23—she was strong, generous and empathetic.

Is there a motto that sums up your philosophy about life?
Life is a fantastic adventure and too short to have regrets.

What advice would you give someone embarking on a legal career?
Be prepared to have the patience to do the hard yards before you reap the benefits.

CONTINUED FROM PAGE 103
- Consistent—give it regularly
- Current—give it soon after performance
- Comprehensive—discuss all aspects
- Candid—be honest and open.

As I stated previously, good managers insist on the bad news, so take time out to elicit feedback from your team. Included in the appendices (E, F and G) are three questionnaires that you can try out as an exercise with your team.

Appendix E is a team performance questionnaire that you can hand out to your team members. Appendix F is a self-assessment questionnaire for supervisees and Appendix G is a self-assessment questionnaire for supervisors to complete. Follow the instructions at the top of each questionnaire and you may be surprised by the results you get!

IDEA #73

BE A SHOULDER TO CRY ON

It will enhance the development of younger lawyers if you can act as a sounding board for them as they make difficult decisions about which career paths to go down. They must understand that planning their future is their responsibility, not their employers'. Perhaps the best piece of advice you could give are the words suggested by David Maister in *True Professionalism*:

> "Do whatever you enjoy. Don't choose something you don't enjoy just because it's what you think we want."

Appendices H and I offers some questions that younger lawyers should consider as they plan their careers.

IDEA #74

GIVE EVERYBODY A BUSINESS CARD

Everyone who works in your firm is an ambassador of the firm. They don't have to be a lawyer to represent the firm. Consequently, everybody should be given a business card for two reasons; first, because it sends out a message to your people that they are not second-class citizens but are an important part of the team; second, your people need to be out there in the community speaking highly of your firm and being in the position to hand out cards to people they meet socially and who might need a lawyer. Before you start thinking about the cost of this exercise, start thinking of the benefits. Think positively.

IDEA #75
CELEBRATE SUCCESSES

In one of my workshops in Melbourne, a lawyer told me that his firm had never celebrated any successes, not because it never had any, but because their people become so wrapped up in the events of the day they rarely took time to reflect on their achievements. Several weeks after this workshop I called him to ask what he had done about it. He said that the firm had paid for all the staff and their partners to go out to dinner at a smart restaurant in town—an exercise that proved to be a major boost to staff morale.

Celebrate your successes and achievements and don't take them for granted. Celebrate when a young lawyer passes his or her Bar exams, when the team wins an important case or negotiates a good settlement for a client, or when someone wins positive publicity for your firm.

IDEA #76
INVITE ALL YOUR STAFF TO AN IN-HOUSE MOTIVATIONAL MOVIE EVERY MONTH

A great way to get staff buzzing and thinking about life's priorities is to show them a motivating movie. My favourite is *Dead Poets' Society* starring Robin Williams as Mr Keating, the teacher out to make a difference in the lives of his students. Approach a local cinema and book the cinema for a private showing. Invite your clients along at the same time.

> *"The human race is filled with passion; and medicine, law, business, engineering—these are noble pursuits and necessary to sustain life; but poetry, beauty, romance and love—these are what we stay alive for."*

MR KEATING

IDEA #77
INVEST MONEY IN YOUR PEOPLE'S PERSONAL AND PROFESSIONAL DEVELOPMENT

Many law societies make it compulsory for lawyers to continue their legal education and to attend a certain number of courses each year. Any self-respecting professional would naturally want to ensure his or her skills are continually being honed. But lawyers need a much wider set of skills to survive the challenges ahead. The ability to present themselves persuasively either in a conversation or from the platform, to negotiate, to communicate in plain language, to coach younger staff, to balance ethical responsibilities with client interests, to close a deal, to mediate, and so on. Firms should be investing a minimum 10% of their annual turnover in education of this nature.

IDEA #78

OFFER STAFF FLEXITIME

This option is increasingly popular, particularly with people who have young children to care for. Flexitime enables staff members to attend to other commitments in life while continuing to practise law. However, where clients need legal advice around the clock, this can be unworkable. A managing partner commented to me recently that flexitime presents the biggest challenge to him as he finds it very difficult to keep abreast of who is working on which particular days. Where there are demanding clients and work is piling up, flexitime needs to be managed carefully.

IDEA #79

REWARD YOUR PEOPLE (AND YOURSELF) WITH MORE TIME OFF

Occasionally, work demands that your people work beyond their fixed hours. When they go the extra mile, it is fair that they should be rewarded for it. Giving time off is an excellent way to acknowledge their efforts and to show appreciation. The boss of the advertising agency I used to work for used to send the female secretaries off to a luxurious, ladies-only health spa for a good half-day pampering. They loved it and the boss paid for it!

EVELYN ASHLEY

Principal, The Red Hot Law Group,
Atlanta, Georgia, USA.

How did you come up with the concept of the Red Hot Law Group?
We focus on companies who are from emerging growth industries such as
high-tech companies who are at an early stage of their development. I have
had a lot of experience with early-stage technology firms who have got red-
hot projects on their hands. It is at the early stages that they need their
lawyers to help them raise cash to get their projects off the ground and
launch their products onto the market.

**I believe the State Bar of Georgia had something to say about your
firm's name?**
Yes, they did! The ethics committee had been inundated with calls from small
firms and older lawyers complaining about our name, The Red Hot Law
Group. Georgia and most of the States have an ethics rule which requires the
name of a licensed attorney to appear in the firm's name. We believe this rule
was derived from the time when communications were not great and so that
the public knew it was dealing with a licensed attorney. Now, after all these
years, you have firms containing the name of dead people!
We deliberately included my surname at the end to keep the ethics
committee happy. When we pointed this out to them, we never heard from
them again!

What would you say is different about your firm?
One of the ways we have structured the firm is to create an environment
with core values for lawyers with a minimum of three years experience.
In traditional firms, you have a hierarchical structure. The people at the
bottom are pressed. They carry responsibility for the people at the top.
We don't do that. We only have partners and associates. We have created a
good environment to attract very good lawyers. We have an "accelerator
company" which takes equity in some of our early-stage company clients.
This option provides all our lawyers with the upside. We have an NA ("no
assholes") policy which embodies our core values—mutual respect,
mutual trust, customer service, teamwork, quality product, integrity and
quality of life. It's not rocket science. We realise we have to be able to
laugh at ourselves.

We offer our clients entrepreneurial education. We are based on pragmatic counselling. We put clients in a position whereby we help them through the process, give them a focus and take the worry out of the equation for them. It's a partnership.

Is there still an adverse public perception of lawyers in the US?
Absolutely. One of the problems is that when the public thinks "lawyer", it thinks litigator. Criminal defence lawyers are considered to be the worst of the worst. One of the other problems is that litigation costs are out of control. The US has been talking for some time about taking steps to amend that part of the law. Until those words are put into action, I think the public will continue to perceive lawyers as people who like to create a dispute.

How can lawyers change adverse perception?
The media is great at drawing attention to the bad things about the profession. Certainly, there are some lousy lawyers out there. However, we are not all like that and I think it is up to the rest of us to develop good relationships with clients so that they think well of us rather than considering us to be a necessary evil.

How important do you consider the contribution of the "behind the scenes" team in a law firm?
It is absolutely critical. Their contribution is overlooked across the professions. I don't think they are adequately rewarded. The legal and accounting professions have a type of club atmosphere in which a class system operates. Lawyers can be very arrogant individuals who consider themselves superhuman. We have tried to change that attitude here through our core values, especially the value of respect. This means we ask everyone to treat everyone else as they would expect to be treated themselves. It is critical for us to grow an environment in which people want to work.

What is your firm's dress code?
We have a couple of lawyers who show up in suits and ties but this is usually because they are visiting clients. We have a relaxed dress code and one of the highs we get is when people visit our offices and comment on how comfortable they feel.

What rewards do you find in your work?

I like to live vicariously though my clients. I can point to a number of companies I have represented and who have gone on to make a good name for themselves. I can say that I was there at the beginning. That's rewarding. Another thing is recently we had two company retreats. One of our new people, who had joined us from a newspaper, came up to me and said she couldn't tell who was the lawyer and who was the non-lawyer! For me, that was rewarding and represented success.

Are lawyers greedy?

Generally, I think they are. When I started out it felt as though I was being hooked up to a machine and money was being siphoned out of me.

What are your views about the role of women in the profession?

I believe women have made lots of inroads, especially at our firm. One of the barriers to their progress has been the traditional model, i.e. you have to get on track and stay with it, do what men do and then become a partner. If you don't then you fall behind. For young women who want to have a family, that is not a good environment. However, flexi hours and accessibility to daycare are making their lives easier.

How do you balance your work and your private life?

I'm not the most balanced person! I have no children but I have a dog who I'm surprised hasn't run away yet! My sense of balance comes through the time I share with my husband, Alan. We both work hard and it consumes everything we do. We have five to eight vacations a year and like to get out of town. We are great walkers and we love to ski and snorkel, too.

What advice do you have for someone embarking on a legal career?

I mentor lots of young people. I say to them, "Understand what you are getting into". Do other work before you undertake law school. It is important that people make choices and I'm not convinced that people between the ages of 15 and 21 know what they are meant to do. I'd suggest that if they are thinking of a career in law they should cold call a few lawyers and ask what their day is like. If their answers excite, then maybe law is the right choice.

If you could choose, would you do it all over again?

Yes. I waited 10 years to do this. I wanted to be different and since making my decision to be a lawyer, I've had a ball.

Do you have a favourite motto?

Yes, it is one we use with our entrepreneur clients: "He who has the gold makes the rules".

CHAPTER 6

Connecting with Life

"Live and work, but do not forget to play, to have fun in life and really enjoy it."

EILEEN CADDY

After I had been working as a lawyer in London for a few years, the absurdity of my everyday existence struck me one morning as I travelled to work on the London Underground. It would normally take me on average an hour to travel from door to door to get to and from work. That meant two hours a day, five days a week (10 hours), 48 weeks a year (480 hours), allowing for holidays, spent commuting. I was 27 years old. I thought to myself that if I continued in this way until retirement at age 65 (38 years away), I would spend 480 hours a year commuting to work. That is 18,240 hours, 760 days or just over two years of my life.

The prospect horrified me. I used to stare at posters on the Underground advertising exotic places in the sun. I knew then that there were other things I wanted to do with my life than live in London and commute to work.

My lifestyle these days is far removed from all that. I live in a beautiful, sub-tropical part of Australia. Most mornings I walk the beach and sometimes swim. I sometimes think back to the hundreds of thousands of people stuck in traffic jams, losing their tempers and getting stressed even before they have arrived at their workplace. Some people say I'm lucky. I don't consider myself to be lucky, although I do think I am fortunate to have appreciated that I had a choice in life. Difficult decisions have had to be made about what I do and where I live. What is important to me is quality of life and often the finest things in life are free—the walks along the beach, the sunsets, the sound of birdsong in the morning.

Most people, I think, enjoy these things and the older they get, the more they recognise that happiness does not come from external factors such as bigger and better cars and houses. Happiness comes from within.

We have no idea how long we have on this planet; if we are lucky we'll live to over 80. If we are unlucky, we may not see the sunrise tomorrow. So the challenge is to make the best use of our time so we can achieve—and enjoy.

THE THREE Ps

As you figure out what your priorities are in life and how you can enjoy it more, think about three criteria which, when they coincide, will give you personal and professional fulfilment. The three criteria are represented by the three circles opposite:

- Professional skills and talent
- Purpose
- Passion

To make my point, allow me to reflect on my own experience just one more time.

PROFESSIONAL SKILLS AND TALENT
Traditionally, for many lawyers (and most people in life), making full use of their professional skills and talent represents success. Achieving a reputation as a professional is, for many, what life is all about. Certainly, that was how I thought as a young lawyer.

After practising law for nearly five years, I could probably have put a tick in the circle and at that stage in my career, I would have said that I was using my professional skills and ability well. I enjoyed the advocacy aspect of my work. My reputation was good, even though I was relatively inexperienced.

PURPOSE
However, I knew something was missing. For example, I never felt good about getting someone off who, in all probability, was guilty. Even on a guilty verdict, I never felt I was making much of a contribution to society or assisting my client in the long term by simply presenting mitigation on his or her behalf. I felt I was doing something that had little purpose or meaning for me.

PASSION
Not only that, I didn't feel passionate about the work I was doing. Apart from the collegiate feeling and social life shared with my professional

colleagues, the work really wasn't that much fun. Most of my clients were difficult and often unpleasant to deal with.

The challenge for everyone in life is to be able to put a tick in each of the three circles; to use their professional skills and talents to the maximum, to do something that has a purpose and meaning, and to do something they feel passionate about and which is fun. Sadly, many people who have the freedom and opportunity to make something of their lives can't put a tick in any one circle. How many circles can you put a tick in?

Here are some further ideas to help you towards putting a tick in each of the three circles:

IDEA #80
SET GOALS

One of the most common complaints expressed by lawyers is that they feel they do not have enough time. Many of them are dreaming of a day with 30 hours in it. They don't exist and even if they did, those lawyers would be wishing there were then 40 hours in every day. The challenge is to make the best use of the 24 hours we all share so a healthy balance is struck between work and play. Start by setting some personal goals before you make a business plan. Decide what you want for yourself and your family and then build a business and financial plan designed to meet those objectives.

You might want to set goals that relate to free time, holidays, fitness, diet, home renovation, or any number of interests or passions you want to pursue. Once you have decided what you want, plan when you want it by and how you are going to pull it off. How many of us make New Year's resolutions only to find ourselves halfway into the year having achieved none of them?

There are many books out there that will help you develop your personal, financial and business goals. The important thing to remember is to plan your work and work your plan. Write down your goals, make a plan, do it and review your progress continually.

Commit to being successful and develop an attitude of "I am happy, prosperous, healthy and I enjoy life". Then live that way.

IDEA #81

GET YOURSELF A COACH

A coach is an independent, qualified person who can partner you and push you towards achieving your goals. This person acts as your conscience, making sure you do what you say you'll do. Your coach can also give you an objective view about how you are running your life. Ensure the person you choose is not just a mentor, i.e. someone who you admire and respect, but someone who you will allow to keep at your heels, just like a sporting coach.

IDEA #82

HAVE A WHITEBOARD ON YOUR OFFICE WALL

I have one in my office that is divided into six columns. Work-in-Progress, Administration, Long-term Projects, Prospects, To Do Today, and To Do This Week. It helps me to prioritise tasks that need attention and to maintain a balanced focus between long-term goals and short-term priorities.

IDEA #83

CLEAR OFFICE CLUTTER

Many lawyers' offices are more often untidy than tidy. Files are piled up high and there are papers all over the desk. How anyone can operate efficiently in this environment is a mystery to me. If your office is a mess, start clearing it up—now! Robyn Pearce is a leading time management specialist and author of *Getting a Grip on Time* (Reed Publishing, 1996). Here are her top tips to help you clear the clutter in your office.

1. Find a place for everything and put everything in its place
2. The space closest to your work station is the most precious—don't clutter it with junk
3. File everything alphabetically (or use some other consistent system)
4. Keep unnecessary material out of sight—otherwise it's physical graffiti
5. Make the decision once about where to put a piece of paper, and write on the top right corner
6. Computer systems follow the same basic principles
7. Store things upright, not flat. They're easier to find the next time
8. Archive systematically—every year
9. Label everything
10. Throw out stuff you don't need. Ask yourself these key questions: Will I ever need this again? If I do, where can I get it from if I throw this away? What's the worst thing that can happen if I throw this out? When

was the last time I used it?

11. Have a parking place for everything, even keys and glasses. Then you'll never lose things

12. Create a "halfway to the rubbish bin" file for the things you can't throw out—yet

13. Use periodical boxes (and manilla folders for sub-categories) to store loose paper upright

14. Label boxes and files as you go—don't rely on memory

15. DO IT NOW!! Don't look at something and put it aside for later. If possible, act immediately. If you have time to handle it you've usually got time to do it, or at least move it one stage further.

IDEA #84

GET OUT OF BED HALF AN HOUR EARLIER EACH DAY AND GO FOR A WALK

A couple of years ago, I had a good look at myself in the mirror naked. It wasn't a good look! My body wobbled in all the wrong places when I jumped up and down. I decided to change it and made some choices about my routine. The first thing I decided to do—and continue to do wherever I am—was get up half an hour earlier and go for a walk. I started to walk just four kilometres every morning. This, combined with minor adjustments to my diet, led to a weight and wobble loss of 12 kilos in just five weeks. An early morning walk is not only is it good for your body, it also helps clear your mind for the day ahead.

IDEA #85

LISTEN TO TAPES ON YOUR WAY TO WORK

When you travel to the office in the morning, whether by car or public transport, make the most of your time by listening to a business audio tape. There are thousands on the market, all offering useful information on how you can be more successful in life.

> *"Learning is the beginning of wealth.*
> *Learning is the beginning of health.*
> *Learning is the beginning of spirituality.*
> *Searching and learning is where the miracle process begins."*

JIM ROHN

IDEA #86
READ MORE
Don't say you haven't got time to read. Make it a priority in your day and you will have the time! Successful people are learners and they get their information and inspiration from listening to tapes and reading books; not just business or self-help books but also novels, newspapers and magazines.

IDEA #87
KEEP A JOURNAL
For the past few years, I have kept a journal in which I write down goals, dreams, experiences and accomplishments. I review what I have written from time to time and when I do so, I am reminded of how much I have achieved or learnt since.

IDEA #88
HAVE A MIDDAY MASSAGE
You can't take care of your clients if you don't take care of yourself. That is why exercise and diet is such an important part of being successful. Remedial massage is another great way to alleviate stress. There are many types of remedial or relaxation massages, such as Shiatsu, Swedish, Thai and Kahuna, to name just a few. Ask your masseur or masseuse what would be best for you.

Many firms now have mobile masseurs visit their offices to give their staff a neck and shoulder massage while they're at their desks. This is a step forward, but not half as effective as having a 60-minute session away from the office. Make an appointment with your masseur, put it in your diary and do not cancel it unless under exceptional circumstances. Treat the appointment with your masseur as if it was with a client.

IDEA #89
SCHEDULE A NON-OFFICE DAY
In spite of the high levels of dissatisfaction in the legal profession, there are some happy lawyers around. Larry Schreiter, author of *The Happy Lawyer*, is one. His solution to getting out of the office more often is to schedule all Fridays as non-office days. He is in the driving seat and in control of his career. His career isn't controlling him. Try it for yourself! Schedule some non-office time in your diary and commit yourself to it.

IDEA #90
LEAVE THE OFFICE NO LATER THAN 5.30PM
If that is what you want, then make a commitment to leave the office by that time. All you have to do is to choose and make it a priority. You'll be amazed at how it transforms your life. So long as you get the job done for clients, it doesn't really matter how early you leave the office.

Demanding schedules for lawyers are almost unavoidable, so it is important to put the tools in place to ensure you maximise your effectiveness and enjoyment both at work and at home. You can do this! The following two ideas are courtesy of Karen Beard, a New Zealand-based corporate wellness specialist. They will help you to make positive lifestyle changes so that you can invest in your health and your practice. After all, the time to take care of your health is now while you have it, not in 20 years time when you're lying in a hospital bed. In the past, too much of our attention to health and wellness has been reactive rather than preventative, and the legal profession is one of the worst for the crash and burn syndrome.

IDEA #91
KEEP ON MOVING
Ensure you are up and moving on your feet for at least one hour each day. That means taking the stairs, parking the car further away from the office, walking to appointments, and leaving the office to buy your own sandwich at lunchtime. Researchers from the University of Pittsburgh have proven that four daily 10-minute walking sessions have almost the same cardio-vascular fitness gains, and creates almost the same fat losses, as continuous physical activity.

IDEA #92
KNOW WHEN AND HOW TO LET OFF STEAM!
The word stress has a lot of negative connotations but it is not always bad. We can all take a certain amount of stress, we just need to know where our limit is before we blow the lid off the pressure cooker. Stress only becomes bad when you ignore the warning signs that you are overdoing things, e.g. fatigue, early-morning wakening, skin rashes, upset stomach, diarrhoea, headaches, trouble in relationships at home and at work, workaholic attitude, inability to relax, and so on.

SURVIVAL TIPS FOR STAYING SANE

- Move for at least one hour a day
- Put parallel lines in your diary blocking out time to move and/or exercise—enter it as a meeting so you cannot change it
- Make sure you have tiny pockets of quiet time throughout your day to allow your mind to be still and get creative
- Meditate daily
- Eat five small meals per day
- Eat balanced food most of the time, but still enjoy your food and the social ritual that surrounds meals
- Drink at least eight glasses of water a day
- Limit tea and coffee to two to three cups a day
- Have two alcohol-free days a week, no more than 14 drinks total
- Re-introduce into your life the things you love to do but stopped because you got too busy
- Ask for help when you need it
- Make sure that at least one weekend a month you can wake up on a weekend and choose how you would like to spend your time without having committed it all
- Spend time with your family and loved ones
- Look for the little miracles that happen daily, instead of saying you are too busy to stop and take notice

(Reproduced with kind permission of Karen Beard, Corporate Wellness Specialist, The Body Corporate Ltd.)

IDEA #93
SURROUND YOURSELF WITH POSITIVE PEOPLE

Negative people drain you of energy and enthusiasm. They scoff at others' success and achieve little of any value for others or for themselves. They find comfort in saying "It can't be done." Nearly 100 years ago, the citizens of Kitty Hawk signed a petition to have Orville and Wilbur Wright incarcerated in an asylum for inviting the whole town to watch their plane fly! Only five people turned up to witness one of the most important events of the last century. Surround yourself instead with people who are enthusiastic, who believe in you and support you and who share your positive approach to life. You will find you feed off each other's energy.

IDEA #94

BECOME A GOOD LISTENER

Listening is a crucial communication skill, along with speaking and observing. The truth is that listening is a skill and not too many people are good at it. Most people are too busy talking and expressing their point of view rather than actively listening to understand the other person's point of view. You need to listen all the time, to your family, your friends, your clients, your colleagues and, of course, yourself. Take a moment to reflect on your own listening skills; do you let people finish their sentences or do you interrupt and sometimes finish their sentences off for them? Being a good listener will make other people around you feel special, acknowledged and respected.

One technique I use to help me to listen more in a conversation is to imagine there is a "speakometer" that records the percentage of air time a particular person is taking up in a conversation. This is a bit like the television graphic shown during a football game to illustrate who has possession of the ball most. Your challenge is to have the lowest percentage of speaking time. The people who have the highest are boring.

Listening is not the same as hearing. Listening requires you to be very present and to absorb everything that is being said to you. Five things you might try are:

- Look at the people speaking to you
- Be interested
- Be sincere
- Contribute to the conversation
- Maintain eye contact (i.e. don't look over their shoulder and plan on who to speak with next).

IDEA #95

LEARN TO MEDITATE

Meditation can create a deep sense of relaxation in your mind and body. It quietens the mind although it remains awake throughout. Try following these simple steps:

1. Find a quiet place and sit in a comfortable position
2. Close your eyes
3. Breathe normally but focus on your breathing throughout

4. If your mind wanders, gently bring back your focus to your breathing
5. Do this for 15 minutes
6. At the end, keep your eyes closed for a couple of minutes and allow yourself to recover. This technique will help you to feel deeply relaxed.

IDEA #96
DO SOMETHING CREATIVE
Lawyers aren't always perceived as being creative people, yet I have met many who are. They play musical instruments, they dance, paint, write, sing, or act. Many are brilliant after-dinner speakers. Perhaps there is some creative energy inside you that's dying to escape? If so, why not let it out?

IDEA #97
GET COMFORTABLE WITH WHO YOU ARE
Some people I have met find it difficult to look at themselves long and hard in the mirror. They don't always like the person (not just the physical reflection) staring back. I recite these verses occasionally at my seminars and it seems to touch many people:

When you get what you want in your struggle for self
And the world makes you king for a day
Then go to the mirror and look at yourself
And see what that man has to say

For it isn't a man's father, mother or wife
Whose judgment upon him must pass
The fellow whose verdict counts most in his life
Is the man staring back from the glass

He's the fellow to please, never mind all the rest
For he's with you right up to the end
And you know you've passed your most difficult test
If the man in the glass is your friend

You can fool the whole world down the pathway of years
And get pats on the back as you pass
But your final reward will be heartache and tears
If you've cheated the Man in the Glass.

FROM THE AUSTRALIAN WELLBEING ANNUAL

IDEA #98

LAUGH AND SMILE MORE OFTEN

Laughter is a great stress release. You know what amuses you; maybe it is a play, a particular TV program or a comedian. Give yourself more opportunities to laugh. Smiling has a similar effect. When you smile at people, they usually smile back. A smile costs nothing and it makes you and the recipient feel better.

IDEA #99

HAVE SOME PHONE-FREE TIME

In an effort to oblige everyone, you risk serving no-one particularly well. Create some calm in your day and have a certain period of time when you don't take phone calls. This will help you relax and to get more done. Dan Kennedy, who is one of America's most successful marketing experts, only accepts calls once a week at a pre-arranged time. All other times, you have to leave a message if you want to get hold of him!

IDEA #100

MAKE WAY FOR LEISURE TIME

The biggest mistake lawyers make is that they do not give themselves enough quality leisure time. Many say they are too busy working, but you cannot afford not to take leisure time! It is an essential part of life. Without it your work suffers. Remember the saying, "The bow kept forever taut will break"? Leisure allows you to relax, to recharge, to see things in perspective and to think creatively. Leisure should not be an enforced two-week holiday every year, nor should it be just a sabbatical (although that's a good idea) every four years. If you think you don't have time, your work will suffer and so will your relationships.

IDEA #101

EAT MORE BANANAS

You are probably wondering by now why you should eat more bananas! It's because they are good for you. Experts agree that as a quick source of carbohydrate fuel, bananas are better for you than any other fruit. They are great for an energy boost. The essential qualities of a banana should be synonymous with those of a lawyer: they are good for you and they are great value for money!

WHERE TO FROM HERE?

Since leaving the practice of law, I have read many books that have helped me to initiate changes and make improvements to my business and my life. Change can be a frightening prospect. It takes courage to implement new ideas and start doing things differently. We find it relatively easy to embrace technology and make it a part of everyday life, yet we find it difficult to embrace new thinking and make positive changes to our lives. Until we learn to address and overcome our own individual insecurities, not much will change. Most organisations are still run today in the same hierarchical way that they were run 400 years ago. Yet the world is changing and we must learn to adapt. Those who adapt the fastest are those who will benefit the most. It's often said that there are three types of people: those who make things happen, those who watch things happen, and those who wonder what happened.

I believe it is time for the legal profession individually and collectively to make things happen, not just for its own benefit but for the public it serves. By doing so, it will restore public confidence in a profession that has been, and still is, undervalued for the contribution it makes to society. Society will be better off, and so will the lawyers who play their part.

"Every end is a new beginning."

SUSAN HAYWARD

JOHN CLARK

John's career has taken him from legal practice to general management as managing partner of one of New Zealand's leading commercial practices. These days, he spends his time consulting, mentoring, parenting and doing volunteer work. He is also the author of a best-selling book, The Money or Your Life.

Why did you choose law as a career?

I didn't choose law, it happened to me. At school it was assumed that I would go into an honourable profession, and having graduated in law, the most obvious option was to go through the interview process. I got a job and there it was. It was not a conscious choice. It never occurred to me to ask, "What do I enjoy doing?".

Why did you leave the law?

I left because I knew in the first week at law school that it wasn't for me, but it took me 15 years to have the guts to act on my conclusion. During those 15 years, I kept on climbing the ladder. I did a Masters in Law in the US, worked for General Motors in Detroit and Linklaters in London, and then returned to New Zealand and became a partner.

Back then, the firm I worked for was the first "national" firm to be formed in New Zealand. We had a plethora of restructuring to be achieved and as I wasn't interested in law, the outlet for me became management. This was the turning point for me. From 1984 I was on the firm's management committee and in 1986 I was asked to take on the role of managing partner, which meant I had the luxury of being able to make a career transition while remaining within my existing firm.

Subsequently, I took a one-year sabbatical in London to do the Sloan Fellowship at the London Business School. In retrospect, I was hoping management was my thing, but one of the great benefits of the Sloan Program was that I discovered that management wasn't my bliss either. I knew it was a transition, but part of the deal of going to London was that I would serve a further three years as managing partner when I returned to New Zealand.

By the end of 1993, I had a two-year-old daughter and a two-month-old son. It was a good time to take six months off, to stand back from everything and then to relaunch.

The six-month stock-take was immensely rejuvenating. For the first time, I began to think about writing a book. I thought I would do a book on unleashing talent. During my time as managing partner, I had been constantly vexed by the feeling that, although many of my colleagues in the white-collar world were immensely successful, lovely people with big incomes, they were, despite their stellar performance, only operating at 80-90% of their capability.

I decided to write the book and spent about five months researching it. By chance I was sent a video, 'The Power of Myth' by Joseph Campbell, in which he talked about "following your bliss". That phrase deeply resonated with me. I realised that the key to unleashing your talents is to follow your bliss. This became a central theme of my book. Now, when I talk to colleagues and clients, I often ask them whether they are following their bliss. I find that people who are off balance can be helped by asking themselves that question.

Do you believe lawyers are doing enough to advance society?
Increasingly, I believe in the kind of "physician, heal thyself" approach. In my 20s I was a great believer in being involved in movements to change the world. Now I feel the best way for me to influence the world is to get myself in shape. I would like to see lawyers do more to change themselves. It's all about authenticity; living life by being true to who you are.

What can leaders of the profession do to lay the foundations for the future?
As a leader, I sought to be extremely values driven. Many colleagues didn't share my values—they wanted to earn as much money as possible and this caused conflict. I sometimes found myself counselling colleagues and partners who were of great economic value to the firm to leave and follow their bliss, even though that was contrary to the firm's short-term economic interests. I still believe that to have been the right course of action; if people need to leave a firm, or leave the law, to follow their bliss, then so be it. Firms will be more successful if their people truly want to be there.

What are the secrets of your success?
I'm certainly not a paragon. But to the extent that success has come my way, the key has been attention. In life, what comes to you depends on what you give your attention to. Several years before I left the law, I started to give my attention to working out what mattered to me and to founding my life on that. Because I have focused on that type of question, I have kept edging closer to the answer.

Do you welcome the gradual erosion of the divisions between the professions?
I have a neutral view. If clients want it, it's fine by me. I feel some of the big firm mergers are managing partner ego-driven, not client driven. What clients want will ultimately win.

Are lawyers greedy?
Some are and some aren't.

Is there one person who has inspired you beyond any others?
Two people, Joseph Campbell and Charles Handy. Charles taught me at the London Business School and he is as near to a role model for me as anyone. His book 'The Age of Unreason' opened up new horizons for me.

What advice would you offer someone embarking on a legal career?
Be clear as to why you are going into law. Are you doing it to explore? To follow your bliss? To make money? For status? If it is for the first two reasons, then fine. If it is for the latter two, then I fear for you—you may gain money and status, but in the process you may lose yourself.

Appendices

APPENDIX A
STANDARD CLIENT SURVEY LETTER OF INVITATION

A. Client
Any Co
Any Street
Anytown
Any State

Dear Client,

An invitation with a difference!

In an effort to ensure we are providing the levels of service that you expect from the team at Litty Gates & Co, we have engaged **Joe Bloggs**, a consultant, to survey a selection of our valued clients to gauge their perceptions of us. Issues that we wish to address include how effective we are, how valuable our services are to you, and how we can serve you better. We anticipate interviews will take place in July and August of this year.

We would very much appreciate your participation in the survey. This would involve devoting typically anywhere between 30 minutes and one hour to meet with Joe, and to discuss frankly your experiences of your relationship with us and to make any suggestions you might wish on how we can improve our service. Your opinions really do count because without your feedback, we have little idea whether the aspects we focus on are those that you value most as part of our service to you.

Joe has our full authority to carry out this survey and any information he obtains will be solely for the purposes of this survey and will remain confidential as between yourself, Joe Bloggs and ourselves.

We hope you will take part. We are sending you a schedule of Joe's movements so that he and you can plan to meet. Please take a moment to indicate if you would be willing to participate so that he can make the necessary travel arrangements. Should you agree to participate, we would appreciate it if you would spend a few moments completing the enclosed questionnaire in advance of your meeting with Joe, and faxing it directly to him on 123 456 7890. You can also communicate with him at **jbloggs@email.com**

Thank you for your time and your continued business.

Kind regards,

Partner in charge

APPENDIX B
LITTY GATES CLIENT SURVEY FAX BACK FORM

Name..

Organisation ....

City ....

Please indicate if you would be willing to participate in the Litty Gates client survey and be interviewed by Joe Bloggs:

☐ **Yes,** would like to participate

☐ **No,** I regret I won't be able to participate

If you are happy to participate, please indicate 3 dates and times that would be suitable:

1. Date .... Time ....

2. Date .... Time ....

3. Date .... Time ....

Please complete and fax this form to:

Mary Hardcase, Practice Manager at Litty Gates & Co 123 456 7890
by (date) please

APPENDIX C
CONFIDENTIAL CLIENT SERVICE QUESTIONNAIRE

NAME: ....

COMPANY: ....

TITLE: .... DATE: ....

Please indicate your level of satisfaction with each aspect of our service listed below and its importance to you by circling the appropriate number.

The people you dealt with at Litty Gates & Co ...

	How do we perform?		How important is this to you?	
Before the project	*Poor*	*Excellent*	*Not*	*Extremely*
Listened to what you had to say	1 2 3 4 5		1 2 3 4 5	
Demonstrated they understood your concerns	1 2 3 4 5		1 2 3 4 5	
Explained what they would do and why	1 2 3 4 5		1 2 3 4 5	
Explained what it was likely to cost you	1 2 3 4 5		1 2 3 4 5	
Discussed the billing procedure	1 2 3 4 5		1 2 3 4 5	
During the project				
Answered the phone pleasantly and promptly	1 2 3 4 5		1 2 3 4 5	
Were responsive to your enquiries	1 2 3 4 5		1 2 3 4 5	
Delivered what they promised	1 2 3 4 5		1 2 3 4 5	
Kept deadlines	1 2 3 4 5		1 2 3 4 5	
Were accessible	1 2 3 4 5		1 2 3 4 5	
Kept you updated on developments	1 2 3 4 5		1 2 3 4 5	
Kept you updated on likely variations to the cost	1 2 3 4 5		1 2 3 4 5	
Had a high standard of presentation	1 2 3 4 5		1 2 3 4 5	
Were interested in you beyond the specific task	1 2 3 4 5		1 2 3 4 5	
Demonstrated proactivity in their dealings with you	1 2 3 4 5		1 2 3 4 5	
Demonstrated commerciality in their advice	1 2 3 4 5		1 2 3 4 5	
Were up to date on industry issues	1 2 3 4 5		1 2 3 4 5	
Communicated clearly	1 2 3 4 5		1 2 3 4 5	
Related well to you	1 2 3 4 5		1 2 3 4 5	
If unavailable, returned your calls promptly or offered alternative assistance	1 2 3 4 5		1 2 3 4 5	

At completion of the project

Delivered results at agreed upon fees	1	2	3	4	5	1	2	3	4	5
Provided the service you had expected	1	2	3	4	5	1	2	3	4	5
Invoiced you accurately and promptly	1	2	3	4	5	1	2	3	4	5
Sprung no unpleasant surprises	1	2	3	4	5	1	2	3	4	5
Continued to keep you informed about industry developments	1	2	3	4	5	1	2	3	4	5
Continued to involve you in firm activities	1	2	3	4	5	1	2	3	4	5

Comments

What is one change we could make to improve our service?

_____

_____

_____

_____

Are there any other aspects of our service you would like to comment on?

_____

_____

_____

_____

The person with whom you worked most often was:

_____

_____

_____

_____

APPENDIX D
CHECKLIST FOR SUPERVISEES

To help make sure that your supervising partner gives you clear direction, ask these questions whenever you tackle an assignment:

1. How does this project fit into the scheme of things?
   Why am I doing this project?

2. What should the end product look like?

3. How much time do you expect me to spend on it?

4. Is this is priority?

5. When should it be completed by?

6. Where else can I get information or other help?

7. Who is responsible for decisions and liaising with the client?

8. When do you want me to report back to you?

9. Let me see if I have things clear. Here is what I intend to do.
   Is that what you want me to do?

APPENDIX E
TEAM PERFORMANCE QUESTIONNAIRE

Distribute this questionnaire among your team members, ask them to complete it and then discuss the results together.

Overall, how well do you think our team works together

	Non starters			*Dream team*	
	1	2	3	4	5

Specifically, indicate how the team performs in the following areas:-

	You must be joking!			*Without question*	
All the team feel a common sense of purpose	1	2	3	4	5
The team is working towards achieving agreed goals	1	2	3	4	5
All team members contribute and have a role to play	1	2	3	4	5
Team members give each other feedback	1	2	3	4	5
Team meetings are well run and timely	1	2	3	4	5
Team members provide mutual support	1	2	3	4	5
Team members are accountable to each other	1	2	3	4	5
Team morale is high	1	2	3	4	5
The team's got a great coach	1	2	3	4	5
The team is well rewarded	1	2	3	4	5
The team celebrates its successes	1	2	3	4	5

Suggestions for improvement:

_____

_____

_____

_____

_____

_____

_____

_____

_____

_____

APPENDIX F
SELF-ASSESSMENT QUESTIONNAIRE FOR SUPERVISEES

As part of your ongoing professional development, it is important that you take time to reflect on just how you are doing. Try to answer these questions as honestly as you can and then discuss the results with your supervising partner.

How good am I at:

	Novice				Master
Relating to clients	1	2	3	4	5
Finding and keeping clients	1	2	3	4	5
Handling meetings with clients	1	2	3	4	5
Working with colleagues	1	2	3	4	5
Investigating the background to cases	1	2	3	4	5
Explaining the law and giving practical advice	1	2	3	4	5
Negotiating resolution of legal matters	1	2	3	4	5
Drafting legal documents	1	2	3	4	5
Writing letters in plain English	1	2	3	4	5
Moving cases and deals forward	1	2	3	4	5
Balancing ethical and client responsibilities	1	2	3	4	5
Organising files, time and billing	1	2	3	4	5
Keeping a tidy office	1	2	3	4	5
Making a judgment and solving problems	1	2	3	4	5

TOTAL   __ __ __ __ __

Totals

60-70	You're already doing a superb job
40-60	You're doing pretty well, but keep working at it
Less than 40	You need to work on improving your skills

APPENDIX G
SELF-ASSESSMENT QUESTIONNAIRE FOR SUPERVISORS

Answer the following questions for yourself and or ask some junior colleagues to complete a copy of this page based on their impression of you.

How often do I:

	Never		Sometimes		Always
1. Help supervisee to establish career goals	1	2	3	4	5
2. Help supervisee to establish sound work habits	1	2	3	4	5
3. Check supervisee's levels of motivation	1	2	3	4	5
4. Give constructive feedback to supervisee	1	2	3	4	5
5. Ask for feedback from supervisee	1	2	3	4	5
6. Offer helpful guidance to supervisee	1	2	3	4	5
7. Act as a good mentor	1	2	3	4	5
8. Praise and encourage supervisee	1	2	3	4	5
9. Delegate effectively	1	2	3	4	5
10. Hold effective team meetings	1	2	3	4	5

TOTAL   _   _   _   _   _

Totals
45 - 50   You're already doing a fine job as a coach and supervisor!
35 - 45   You're about average
Under 35   You need to do some serious work on your coaching skills

APPENDIX H
PLANNING TO BECOME FOCUSED

Try to answer these questions and build them into your personal development plan. The object of this exercise is to help you to become focused.

Develop your spoken logo—describe in one sentence what you do for clients.
Don't say, "I'm a lawyer at Litty Gates & Co." Think of how you might phrase it so that it gets people sitting up and taking interest.

_____

_____

_____

_____

_____

Say what makes you special or sets you apart from other lawyers who do the same things for their clients.
For example, you might want to be perceived as being different because of the extra care you give your clients, the innovative ideas you present to them, the research that you have done that no-one else has done, or the simple fact that unlike most other lawyers, you discuss your fees clearly in advance and give unconditional guarantees as to the quality of your service.

_____

_____

_____

_____

Identify your strengths and weaknesses.
For example, communication skills, presentation skills, knowledge of your subject, client base, etc.
Strengths: _____

_____

Weaknesses: _____

_____

Identify any external factors/influences beyond your control that (could) impact negatively on your practice.
List any that come to mind.

_____

_____

_____

_____

Where do you want your career to go?
Where do you see yourself three years from now? Describe how successful you see you and your practice as being.

_____

_____

_____

What specific new skills do you plan to acquire or enhance over the next three years?
List the skills (e.g. legal, interpersonal, communication, team, marketing, networking) that you wish to improve.

_____

_____

_____

Where do you want to be in a year from now?
Describe the results you want to have achieved. For example, increase in fees, new client base, new skills, better relationship with supervising partner, published articles, etc.

_____

_____

_____

What are the specific initiatives that you must take to get you there in the next 12 months?
List those activities that must happen if you are to attain your goals this year.

_____

_____

_____

APPENDIX I
HELPFUL QUESTIONS TO ASK YOUNG LAWYERS WHEN COUNSELLING

- What type of work do you think you would like to do? Why?

- What sort of clients would you like to work with? Why?

- What sort of work gives you the most pleasure?

- How would you like to be described at your funeral?

- For what do you want to be admired and by whom?

- As a lawyer, what contribution do you want to make to society and humanity?

- How important is money to you? Why?

- How important is status to you? Why?

- Are there any things that may be holding you back (e.g. fear, family pressures, financial difficulties, lack of self-confidence) that you would like to discuss in confidence?

- How can I help?

BIBLIOGRAPHY

In researching for and writing this book, I have read or referred to the following texts.

The Manager as Coach & Mentor, by Eric Parsloe (Institute of Personnel Management, London 1995)

Managing the Professional Service Firm, by David Maister (Macmillan, 1993)

True Professionalism, by David Maister (Free Press, 1997)

The Money or Your Life, by John Clark (Tandem, 1997)

The Tao of Coaching, by Max Landsberg (HarperCollins, 1996)

The 80 Things You Must Do to Be a Great Boss, by David Freemantle (McGraw-Hill, 1995)

The 7 Habits of Highly Effective People, by Stephen Covey (The Business Library, 1989)

Breaking the Cycle of Failure in Services, by Leonard Schlesinger and James Heskett (Sloane Management Review, Spring 1991)

Quality Management for Legal Practice, by Rosemary Howell and others (The Law Book Company, 1994)

Law Student Supervision, by A. Alexander and J. Smith (Legal Economics, June 1989)

Law Institute Journal (Victoria), May 1998

Practising Certificate Survey, Law Society of NSW (Keys Young) 1998-9

Marketing the Advisors II, by Wheeler Associates/McCallum Layton/emarketing (1999)

The Sydney Morning Herald, August 30, 1997

How to Assign a Task Clearly, by R. W. Feferman (Legal Economics, April 1987)

Lawyers as Teachers—The Art of Supervision, by H. Rose (Law Practice Management, May/June 1995)

Shift Your But, by Ann Andrews (1997)

Spiritual Medicine, by Laurie Levine (Simon & Schuster, 1998)

Creating Loyal Profitable Customers, by Keith Abraham (People Pursuing a Passion, 1999)

Winning Tenders and Proposals for Lawyers, by Peter Barker (PB Marketing & Media Pty Ltd, 1994)

The Seven Spiritual Laws of Success, by Dr Deepak Chopra (Amber-Allen/New World Library, 1994)

Journey into Healing, by Dr Deepak Chopra (Rider Books, 1994)

Incredible Customer Service, by David Freemantle (McGraw-Hill, 1993)

What Customers Like about You, by David Freemantle (Nicholas Brealy, 1998)

The Justice Game, by Geoffrey Robertson (Vintage, 1999)

The E-Myth (Revisited), by Michael Gerber (Harper Business, 1995)

Making it Happen, by Sir John Harvey-Jones (Collins, 1988)

All Together Now, by Sir John Harvey-Jones (William Heinemann, 1994)

How to Master Networking, by Robyn Henderson (Prentice Hall, 1997)

How to Be Happy and Rich on Your Income, by Hans Jakobi (Wealth Dynamics, 1998)

Money, Success and You, by John Keyhoe (Zoetic Inc, 1990)

The Ultimate Marketing Plan, by Daniel S. Kennedy (Bob Adams Inc, 1990)

Professional Services Marketing, by Neil A. Morgan (Butterworth Heinemann, 1991)

Market-Led Strategic Change, by Nigel Piercy (Butterworth Heinemann, 1992)

Up the Loyalty Ladder, by Murray and Neil Raphel (Harper Business, 1995)

Maverick, by Ricardo Semler (Century, 1993)

101 Simple Things to Grow Your Business, by Dottie and Lilly Walters (Crisp Publications, 1996)

Speak and Grow Rich, by Dottie and Lilly Walters (Prentice Hall, 1997)

Million Dollar Consulting, by Alan Weiss (McGraw-Hill, 1998, 1992)

Money Talks, by Alan Weiss (McGraw-Hill, 1998)

Fastcompany Magazine (# 33 and 35)

Think and Grow Rich, by Napoleon Hill (Fawcett, 1960)

Stress Management for Lawyers, by Amiram Elwork (The Vorkell Group, 1997)

The Sun Herald (Sydney) May 21, 2000

The Happy Lawyer, by Larry Schreiter (Shiloh Publications, 1999)

Alternative Careers for Lawyers, by Hilary Mantis (Random House, 1997)

The Lawyer's Career Change Handbook, by Hindi Greenberg (Avon Books, 1998)

The Terrible Truth About Lawyers, by Mark H. McCormack (Morrow, 1987)

The Money or Your Life, by John Clark (Tandem Press, 1997)

Don't Sweat the Small Stuff at Work, by Dr Richard Carlson (Hyperion, 1998)

Getting a Grip on Time, by Robyn Pearce (Reed Publishing, 1996)

The Australian Financial Review, August 25, 2000

A Guide for the Advanced Soul, by Susan Hayward (In Tune books, 1984)

IF YOU ENJOYED THIS BOOK, THEN READ ON!

To help the many people who are continually striving to learn how to succeed professionally and who enjoy reading, we publish a newsletter, *Simon Says*, three times a year. When you become a subscriber to *Simon Says*, you receive:

- a copy of Simon's audio cassette How to Take Good Care of Your Professional Practice
- 3 copies of *Simon Says* each year
- 3 of the best business books specially selected by Simon each year
- a gift certificate valued at $500* (conditions apply) valid for 12 months

all for just AUD$160 incl GST a year

Why not join the many subscribers and start applying the latest business knowledge to your practice and start getting the results you dream about?

To get your free copy or to subscribe, complete the coupon below:

Name ....

Organisation .... Email...

Address...

Postcode .... Tel # .... Fax #..........................

☐   Please send me a free copy of Simon Says

☐   Please sign me up as a Simon Says subscriber

I enclose payment by

☐ Cheque   ☐ Credit Card

                       ☐ Visa   ☐ Mastercard   ☐ Bankcard   ☐ Amex   ☐ Diners

Name on card ....

Card number.. Expiry...

Signature..

Here's all you need to do: Photocopy this page and complete it, then

FAX to (612) 6680 9992

      or

Fold and MAIL to PO Box 159, Byron Bay, NSW 2481, Australia

      or

CALL us on (612) 6680 9991

      or

EMAIL us at stupman@ozemail.com.au

HOW TO BUILD ON IDEAS LEARNT IN THIS BOOK

One of the keys to your professional fulfilment and success is to constantly improve your leadership and communication skills. To that end, Simon Tupman Presentations provides ongoing consulting, coaching and education in the form of seminars, workshops and conference presentations for lawyers and other professionals who want to get ahead.

His topics include:
- How to Master the Art of Presentation
- Who Cares Wins!—staying on top of your profession and your career
- Coaching with Confidence—supervising and delegating effectively
- Professionalism, Purpose and Passion
- Looking For and After High Value Clients

If you and your colleagues need a boost, then take the first step and call us on (612) 6680 9991 or FAX a copy of this page to (612) 6680 9992 for your initial, no-obligation consultation.

☐ Yes, Simon, I would like to take you up on your offer. Please call me to discuss how you can help me and my team implement the ideas you discuss in 'Why Lawyers Should Eat Bananas'.

My key concerns are (please tick box)

☐ How to connect with clients   ☐ How to motivate my team
☐ How to find good people   ☐ How to attract new clients
☐ How to cross sell   ☐ How to escape the office
☐ How to present like a pro   ☐ How to become a leader

My name is . . . .

My firm is . . . .

My postal address is . . . .

My email address is . . . .

My phone number is . . . .